2 Practice Tests
FOR THE COGAT® GRADE 4

- **Grade 4 Level 10 Form 7**
- **2 Full-Length Practice Tests**
- **352 Practice Questions**
- **Answer Key**
- **Sample Questions for Each Test Area**
- **54 Additional Bonus Questions Online**

Nicole Howard

PLEASE LEAVE US A REVIEW!

Thank you for selecting this book.

We'd love to get your feedback on the website where you purchased this book.

By leaving a review, you give us the opportunity to improve our work.

Nicole Howard and the SkilledChildren.com Team

www.skilledchildren.com

Co-authors: Albert Floyd and Steven Beck

First edition.

TABLE OF CONTENTS

INTRODUCTION

The Cognitive Abilities Test (CogAT®) is an assessment of a student's verbal, quantitative, and nonverbal reasoning ability. Administered to grades K-12, the CogAT® is designed to identify gifted students.

Riverside Publishing has developed the Cognitive Abilities Test since 1954.

This book will increase the student's chances of success by providing an overview of the different types of questions for Grade 4, Level 10, Form 7 of the CogAT® test.

Two comprehensive practice tests and their answer key, with clear explanations, are all included in this book to allow students to understand the testing structure and the different types of questions within it.

Additionally, by reading this book, you gain free online access to 54 bonus practice questions. You will find the link and password on the last page of this book.

It is highly recommended to read this introductory section to understand how the CogAT® works.

Which Students Are Eligible to Take the CogAT Level 10?

This book is dedicated to gifted ten-year-old children and therefore focuses on level 10, form 7 of CogAT®.

Most Grade 4 teachers implement CogAT® Level 10 to identify which of their students will benefit from faster curriculum training modules. Used as a starting evaluation, it delivers reasonably accurate results.

When in the School Year Does the CogAT Take Place?

Several school districts choose to implement these tests at the end of the school year for more reliable and accurate results. If you are the parent or teacher of a student who could potentially qualify for this test, you will probably need to consult your school to determine how to enroll a child for this test.

An Overview of the CogAT Level 10

The CogAT® is administered to a group of students at a single time.

There are three autonomous sections of the test, specifically:

1. Verbal testing

2. Nonverbal testing

3. Quantitative testing

These autonomous sections can be used individually, and some students may only be asked to take one or two parts of the test based on the evaluations of their tutors.

Although there are resources that support students prepare for these tests, the content of the CogAT® isn't generally the same content that is seen in the conventional school curriculum, and students will be asked to think creatively to solve certain questions.

The Length and the Complete Format of the Test

The total time given for the three sections of the Level 10 test is 90 minutes (30 minutes for each section).

INTRODUCTION

Tests will vary, depending on the grades that are being assessed, but the Level 10 CogAT® is divided into 176 multiple-choice questions. The questions are categorized as follows:

Verbal Section

- "Sentence completion" has 20 questions.

- "Verbal classification" has 20 questions.

- "Verbal analogies" has 24 questions.

Nonverbal Section

- "Figure matrices" has 22 questions.

- "Paper folding skills" has 16 questions.

- "Figure classifications" has 22 questions.

Quantitative Section

- "Understanding number analogies" has 18 questions.

- "The number series" has 18 questions.

- "Solving number puzzles" has 16 questions.

The total number of questions for these three sections equals 176.

The Test Breakdown

The verbal section of the test is designed to assess a student's vocabulary, ability to solve problems associated with vocabulary, ability to determine word relationships, and their overall memory retention. The verbal section of the Level 10 CogAT® has three subtypes of questions that need to be answered:

1. Sentence Completion: Students are required to select words that accurately complete sentences in this section. This tests their knowledge of vocabulary.

2. Verbal Classification: Students are required to classify words into like groups in this section. They will be given three words that have something in common,

and will be asked to identify a fourth word that completes the set. Each question in this section will have five possible answers for the students to choose from.

3. Verbal Analogies: Students are required to identify analogies. They will be given two words that go together (e.g. "dog" and "mammal") as well as a third, unrelated word. They must pick the most fitting pair for the third word from the answer choices given, based on the logic used for the original pair of words.

The nonverbal section of the test is designed to assess a student's ability to reason and think beyond what they've already been taught. This section includes geometric shapes and figures that aren't normally seen in the classroom. This will force the students to use different methods to try and solve problems. There are also three subtypes of questions that need to be answered in the nonverbal section of the CogAT:

1. Figure Classification: Students are required to analyze three similar figures and apply the next appropriate figure to complete the sequence in this section.

2. Figure Matrices: Students are introduced to basic matrices (2x2 grids) to solve for the missing shapes within them. Three of the four squares will already be filled out, and they must choose which image fills the last square from the options provided. This is similar to the verbal analogies section, except it is now done using shapes instead of words.

3. Paper Folding Skills: Students are introduced to paper folding and will need to ascertain where punched holes in a folded piece of paper would be after the paper is unfolded.

The quantitative section introduces abstract reasoning and problem-solving skills to learners and is one of the most challenging sections in the test. This section is also structured into three different parts:

1. Interpreting a Series of Numbers: Students are required to determine which number or numbers are needed to complete a series that follows a specific pattern.

2. Solving Number Puzzles: Students will need to solve number puzzles and simple equations. They will be provided with equations that are missing a number.

3. Understanding Number Analogies: Students are introduced to number analogies and will be required to determine what numbers are missing from the number sets. This is similar to figure matrices and verbal analogies.

How to Use the Content in This Book

Since the CogAT® is an important test in all students' schooling careers, the correct amount of preparation must be performed. Students that take the time to adequately prepare will inevitably do better than students that don't.

This book will help you prepare your student(s) before test day and will expose them to the format of the test so they'll know what to expect. This book includes:

- Two full-length CogAT® Level 10 practice questionnaires.

- Question examples for teachers/parents to help their students approach all of the questions on the test with confidence and determination.

- Answer key with clear explanations.

Take the time to adequately go through all of the sections to fully understand how to teach this information to younger students. Many of the abstract versions of these questions will be difficult for some students to understand, so including some visual aids during preparation times will be greatly beneficial.

Tips and Strategies for Test Preparation

The most important factor regarding the CogAT® is to apply the time and effort to the learning process for the test and make the preparation periods as stress-free as possible. Although everyone will experience stress in today's world, being able to cope with that stress will be a useful tool. All students will experience varying amounts of anxiety and stress before these types of tests, but one of the ways to adequately combat this is by taking the time to prepare for them.

The CogAT® has difficult questions from the very beginning. Some of the questions will range from difficult to very abstract, regardless of the age group or level.

It's necessary to encourage your students to use different types of strategies to answer questions that they find challenging.

Students will get questions incorrect in some of the sections, so it's vital to help younger students understand what errors they made so they can learn from their mistakes.

Before You Start Test Preparation

There are multiple factors that may stress students out, regardless of their age and maturity levels. It's imperative for you as an educator to help your students cope with the anxiety and stress of upcoming tests. The tests themselves are going to be stressful, but there are other, external factors that can increase the amounts of stress that children experience.

The first aspect that needs to be focused on is teaching the learners how to deal with stress. Breathing techniques are important, and having a quiet place to use when studying is imperative to decreasing the amount of stress that students experience.

There are other aspects that can help alleviate stress, like teaching your students what pens and pencils they need to bring on the test day and how to successfully erase filled out multiple-choice questions on the test questionnaire.

.

PRACTICE TEST 1 VERBAL BATTERY

This section is designed to assess a student's vocabulary, ability to solve problems associated with vocabulary, ability to determine word relationship and memory retention.

Verbal Analogies

A verbal analogy traces a similarity between a pair of words and another pair of words.

Example

wide $\rightarrow$ narrow : graceful $\rightarrow$

A clumsy   **B** new   **C** honest   **D** tired   **E** old

- First, identify the relationship between the first pair of words.
- How do the words "wide" and "narrow" go together?

The opposite of "wide" is "narrow".

- Now, look at the word "graceful".
- Which of the possible choices follows the previous rule?

The opposite of "graceful" is "clumsy", so the correct answer is A.

Tips for Solving Verbal Analogies

- Try to identify the correlation between the first two words.
- Review all answers before you make a choice.
- Remove any word in the answers that don't have a comparable kind of relationship.
- Also, evaluate the possible alternative meanings of the words.

1.

gold → metal : hydrogen →

A liquid   **B** gas   **C** fabric   **D** rock
E drink

2.

four → number: inch →

A meter   **B** hour   **C** unit   **D** centimeter
E weight

3.

minute → second: day →

A yard   **B** month   **C** gram   **D** hour   **E** mile

4.

temperature → Celsius : weight →

A millimeter   **B** gram   **C** year   **D** degree
E inch

5.

teeth → chew : nose →

A sniff   **B** eat   **C** walk   **D** smoke   **E** taste

6.

cm → centimeter: mm →

A meter   **B** milligram   **C** millimeter   **D** kilogram
E mile

7.

lemon → sour : candy →

A salty   **B** spicy   **C** fruity   **D** sweet   **E** bitter

8.

water → flow : smoke →

A billow   **B** sniff   **C** sink   **D** bounce   **E** creak

9.

arc ⟶ circle : line segment ⟶

A circle **B** line **C** rectangle **D** parallel **E** square

10.

colossal ⟶ immense: cordial ⟶

A safe **B** superior **C** kind **D** huge
E little

11.

fear ⟶ courage : floor ⟶

A wall **B** ceiling **C** door **D** tile **E** marble

12.

fog ⟶ hail : yellow ⟶

A rain **B** flower **C** banana **D** red **E** color

13.

window → wall : engine →

A house   **B** plane   **C** table   **D** computer   **E** door

14.

fruit → apple : planet →

A sky   **B** universe   **C** star   **D** sun   **E** Jupiter

15.

vertebrate → human : invertebrate →

A cat   **B** hen   **C** bear   **D** dog   **E** worm

16.

Nigeria → Africa: Germany →

A Asia   **B** Australia   **C** Europe   **D** North America
E South America

17.
corn → cob : pea →

A bean   **B** banana   **C** pod   **D** garden   **E** seed

18.
accidental → intentional : blunt →

A sharp   **B** white   **C** smooth   **D** true   **E** dull

19.
eyes → see : feet →

A walk   **B** buy   **C** think   **D** taste   **E** create

20.
pedal → bicycle : hard drive →

A smartphone   **B** hair dryer   **C** iron   **D** computer
E car

21.
giraffe → mammal : spider →

A insect **B** arachnid **C** fish **D** reptile **E** mammal

22.
engine → car : tree →

A leaf   **B** forest   **C** garden   **D** field   **E** flower

23.
stooped → posture : slurred →

A music **B** action **C** fear **D** honesty **E** diction

24.
artificial → natural : body →

A flesh **B** youthfulness **C** soul **D** legs **E** man

Verbal Classification

Verbal classification questions ask the student to choose the voice that belongs to a group of three words.

Example

fennel, radish, beet

A banana   **B** apple   **C** pear   **D** blueberries   **E** asparagus

First, identify the relationship between the three words in the first row.
What do the words fennel, radish, beet have in common?

Fennel, radish, beet are all vegetables.

- Now, look at the five worlds: banana, apple, pear, blueberries, and asparagus. Which word goes best with the three words in the top row?

Asparagus are also vegetables, so the correct answer is E.

Tips for Solving Verbal Classification Questions

- Try to identify the correlation between the three words in the top row.
- Review all answers before you make a choice.
- Remove every word in the answers that don't have any kind of relationship with the three words in the top row.
- Also, evaluate the possible alternative meanings of the words.

1.

constitutional, congregational, constructivism

A cartography   **B** church   **C** congratulation
D car   **E** cannibal

2.

democracy, oligarchy, dictatorship

A relativism   **B** monarchy   **C** nobility   **D** city
E civilization

3.

acute, right, obtuse

A high   **B** grease   **C** straight   **D** parallel
E crooked

4.

Aries, Taurus, Gemini

A Virgo   **B** Mars   **C** Moon   **D** Sunday   **E** California

5.

alexandrite, amber, zircon

A gold   **B** silver   **C** turquoise   **D** stone
E myrrh

6.

non-verbal, verbal, written

A invisible   **B** festive   **C** expired   **D** delayed
E visual

7.

hydrogen, fluorine, helium

A neon   **B** beryllium   **C** strontium   **D** barium
E radium

8.

gravitational, chemical, radiant

A colorful   **B** white   **C** warm   **D** elastic   **E** cold

9.

natural, whole, rational

A artificial   **B** previous   **C** true   **D** real   **E** full

10.

duodenum, appendix, colon

A rectum   **B** medulla   **C** heart   **D** cerebellum
E brain

11.

Bronx, Brooklyn, Manhattan

A Pasadena   **B** Westside   **C** Knowsley   **D** Sefton
E Staten Island

12.

Icelandic, Strombolian, Plinian

A Hawaiian   **B** Italian   **C** terrible   **D** Danish
E flaming

13.
hurricane, tornadoes, tsunamis

A thunderstorms   **B** rain   **C** snowfall   **D** wind
E winter

14.
maroon, scarlet, crimson

A lemon   **B** gold   **C** cerise   **D** lime   **E** cyan

15.
almonds, hazelnuts, pecans

A apples   **B** pears   **C** pistachios   **D** coconut
E melon

16.
said, got, took

A saw   **B** see   **C** buy   **D** control   **E** sell

17.
carbohydrates., proteins, fats

A butter   **B** meat   **C** fruits   **D** vitamins   **E** oil

18.
rectangle, rhombus, square

A circle   **B** trapezoid   **C** triangle   **D** cone
E sphere

19.
Zebra Longwing, Ulysses, Blue Clipper

A king   **B** son   **C** fly   **D** spider   **E** Monarch

20.
tractors, seeders, balers

A plows   **B** garden   **C** seeds   **D** car   **E** bike

Sentence Completion

Complete the phrase using the appropriate word that best fits the meaning of the sentence as a whole.

Example

English is the most preferred language of _____ in the world.

A communication   **B** disintegration   **C** war   **D** warriors   **E** criminals

- First, read the sentence. You will realize that one word is missing.
- Look at the answer choices under the main sentence. Which word would go better in the phrase?

Communication= the imparting or exchanging of information by speaking, writing, or using some other medium. Therefore, the right choice is "A".

Tips for Sentence Completion

- First, read the incomplete phrase.
- Think about what type of word you can use and try to anticipate the answer.
- Remove every word in the answers that don't have any kind of relationship with the main sentence.
- Read the incomplete sentence again.

1.

A dictionary is a book or _____ resource that lists the words of a language and gives their meaning.

A close   **B** old   **C** extreme   **D** chemical
E electronic

2.

The sun provides the light and energy that sustains life on earth and its _____ position relative to the earth's axis determines the terrestrial seasons.

A changing   **B** previous   **C** new   **D** obligatory
E parallel

3.

When you change money, you exchange it for the same amount of money in a _____ currency, or in smaller notes, bills, or coins.

A equal **B** different **C** old **D** strange **E** honest

4.

We use capital letters to _____ the beginning of a sentence and we use full stops to mark the end of a sentence

A change   **B** eliminate   **C** mark   **D** delete
E join

5.

The dentist begins by asking the patient some questions about the toothache, including the types of foods that make the pain _____, whether the tooth is sensitive to temperature.

A better   **B** nice   **C** worse   **D** big   **E** delicious

6.

One of the most widely recognized animal _____ in human culture, the lion has been extensively depicted in sculptures and paintings, on national flags, and in contemporary films and literature.

A ghost   **B** statue   **C** painted   **D** symbols
E fantastic

7.

An element is a chemical substance made up of a particular kind of atom and hence cannot be broken down or transformed by a _____ reaction into a different element.

A electric   **B** colorful   **C** nuclear   **D** liquid
E chemical

8.

My tent has to protect against wind, water and snow to _____ a warm and dry climate inside.

A maintain   **B** eliminate   **C** cover   **D** destroy
E excite

9.

Tornadoes come in many shapes and sizes, and they are often _____ in the form of a condensation funnel originating from the base of a cumulonimbus cloud.

A invisible   **B** visible   **C** destroyed   **D** pushed
E hidden

10.

A transitive verb requires a direct object, which is a noun, pronoun, or noun phrase that _____ the verb and indicates the person or thing that receives the action of the verb.

A precedes   **B** follows   **C** creates   **D** moves
E moves

11.

A star glows due to thermonuclear fusion of hydrogen into helium in its core, releasing energy that travels _____ the interior of the star and then radiates outward into space.

A under   **B** over   **C** next   **D** back   **E** through

12.

Mountains are generally less preferable for human habitation than lowlands, because of _____ weather and little level ground suitable for agriculture.

A harsh   **B** hot   **C** humid   **D** tropical   **E** sunny

13.

The Arctic has been warming at three times the global average as a result of climate _____ in Canada.

A stabilization **B** destruction **C** lock **D** change
E cooling

14.

Access to _____ water is often taken for granted, especially in developed countries that have build sophisticated water systems for collecting, purifying, and delivering water.

A hot **B** polluted **C** pure **D** useless **E** bottled

15.

The _____ and structure of leaves vary considerably from species to species of plant, depending largely on their adaptation to climate.

A shape **B** water **C** heat **D** creation **E** warmth

16.

Typically, war becomes intertwined with the _____ and many wars are partially or entirely based on economic reasons.

A pollution   **B** catering   **C** entertainment
D economy   **E** agriculture

17.

Unlike humans, horses do not sleep in a solid, unbroken period of time, but take many _____ periods of rest.

A long   **B** short   **C** high   **D** fun   **E** nice

18.

The brains of humans and other primates contain the same structures as the brains of other mammals, but are generally larger in proportion to _____ size.

A heart   **B** body   **C** leg   **D** foot   **E** arm

19.

A _____ leg is an artificial leg that is used to replace one that has been lost.

A wooden   **B** rubber   **C** lower   **D** prosthetic
E remote controlled

20.

Today, Africa contains 54 countries, most of which have borders that were _____ during the era of European colonialism.

A destroyed   **B** drawn   **C** contaminated
D wasted   **E** improved

PRACTICE TEST 1 NON VERBAL BATTERY

This section is designed to assess a student's ability to reason and think beyond what they've already been taught. This section includes geometric shapes and figures that aren't normally seen in the classroom.

Figure Matrices

Students are provided with a 2X2 matrix with the image missing in one cell. They have to identify the relationship between the two spatial shapes in the upper line and find a fourth image that has the same correlation with the left shape in the lower line.

Example

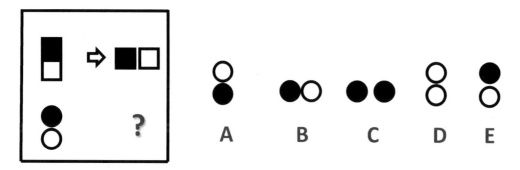

In the upper left box, the image shows a white square and a black square. In the upper right box, the image shows the same squares, but now the white square is to the right of the black square.

The lower left box shows a black circle and a white circle. Which answer choice would go with this image in the same way as the upper images go together?

The image of the answer choice must show two circles; the white circle must be to the right of the black circle.
The right answer is "B".

Tips for Figure Matrices

- Consider all the answer choices before selecting one.
- Try to use logic and sequential reasoning.
- Eliminate the logically wrong answers to restrict the options.
- Train yourself to decipher the relationship between different figures and shapes.

1.

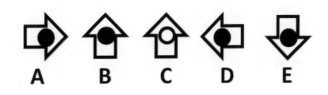

2.

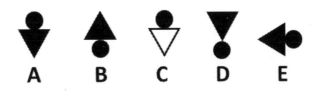

3.

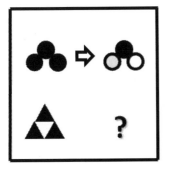

4.

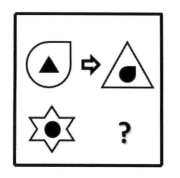

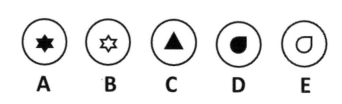

5.

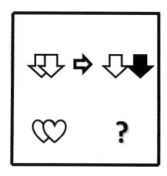

6.

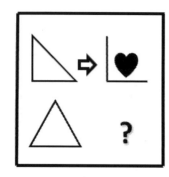

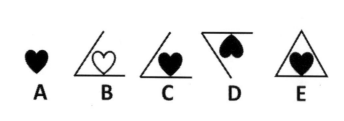

7.

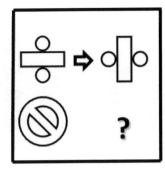

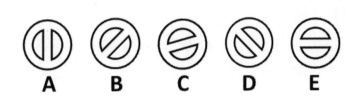

8.

9.

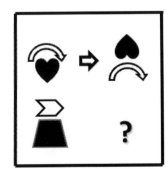

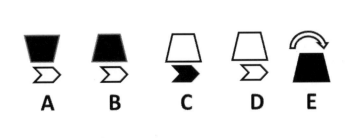

10.

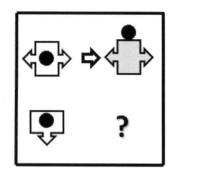

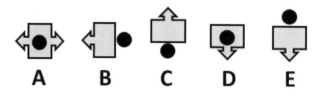

11.

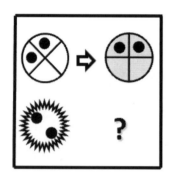

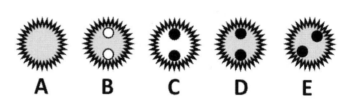

12.

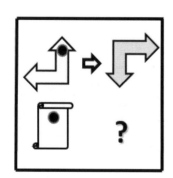

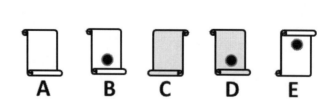

13.

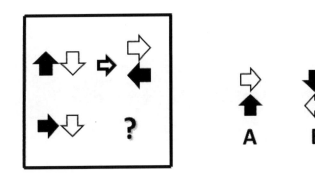

14.

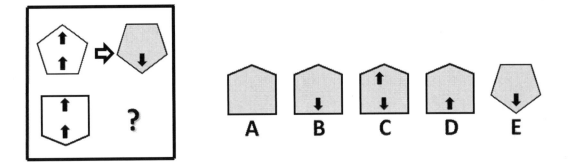

15.

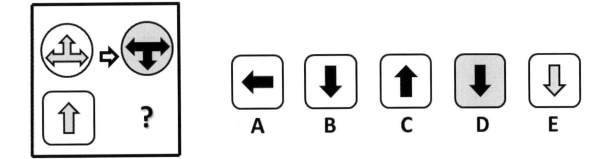

16.

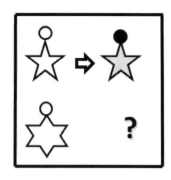

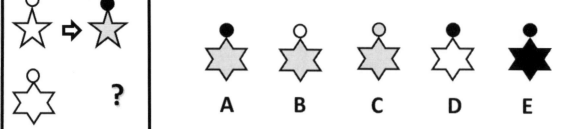

17.

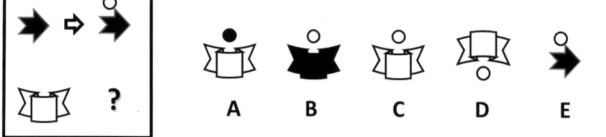

18.

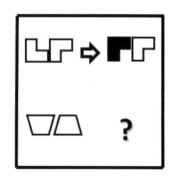

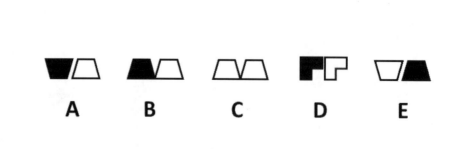

19.

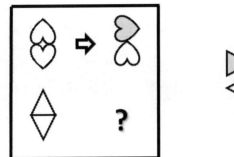

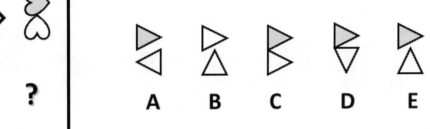

20.

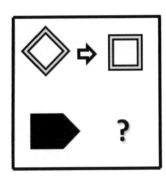

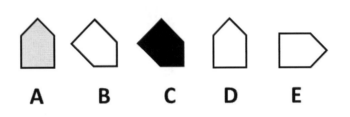

21.

22.

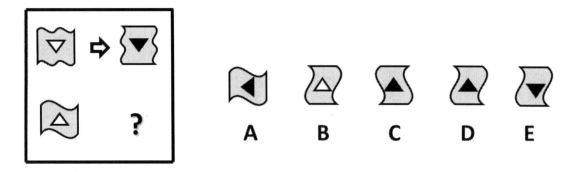

Figure Classification

Students are provided with three shapes and they have to select the answer choice that should be the fourth figure in the set, based on the similarity with the other three figures. The intention is to test the student's ability to recognize similar patterns and to make a rational choice.

Example

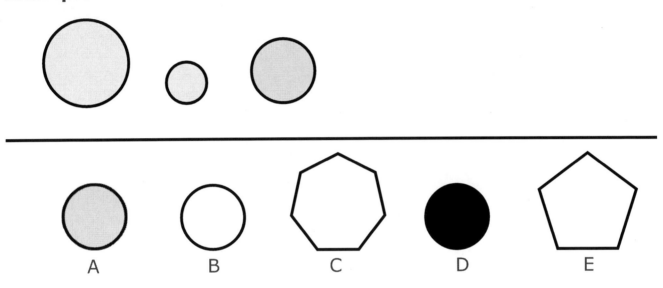

Look at the three pictures on the top. What do these three figures have in common?
You can see three grey circles.
Now, look at the shapes in the row of the answer choices. Which image matches best the three shapes in the top row?

The image of the answer choice must be a grey circle. The right answer is "A".

Tips for Figure Classification

-   Be sure to review all answer choices before selecting one.
-   Try to use logic and sequential reasoning.
-   Try to exclude the obviously wrong options to reduce the answer choices.

1.

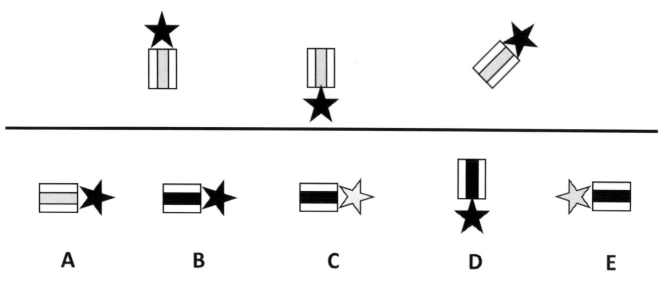

A   B   C   D   E

2.

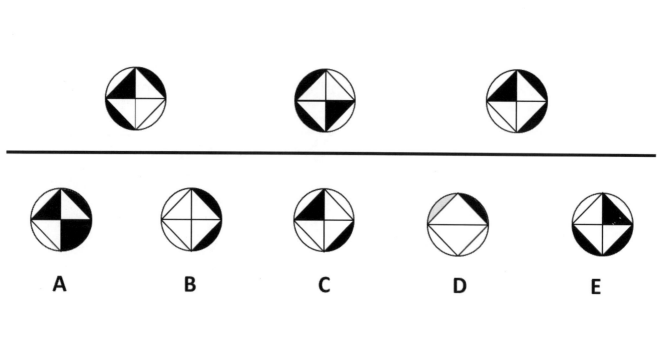

A   B   C   D   E

3.

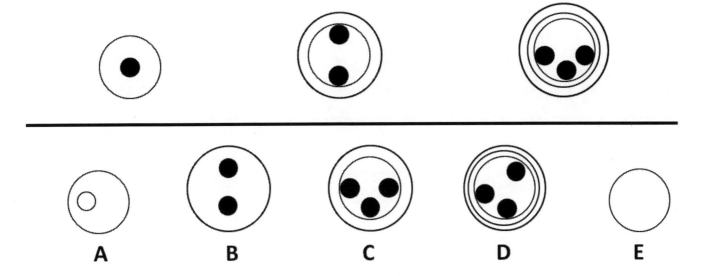

4.

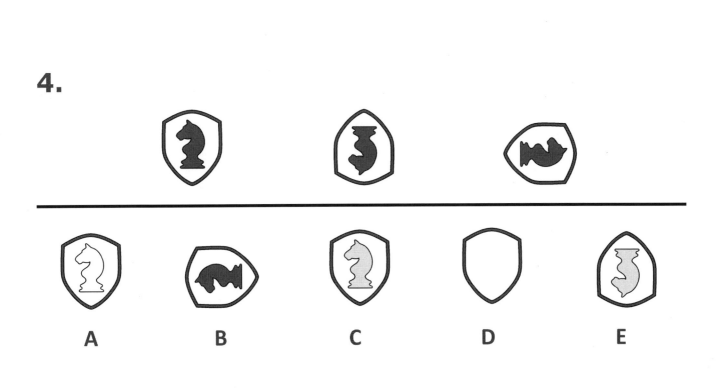

5.

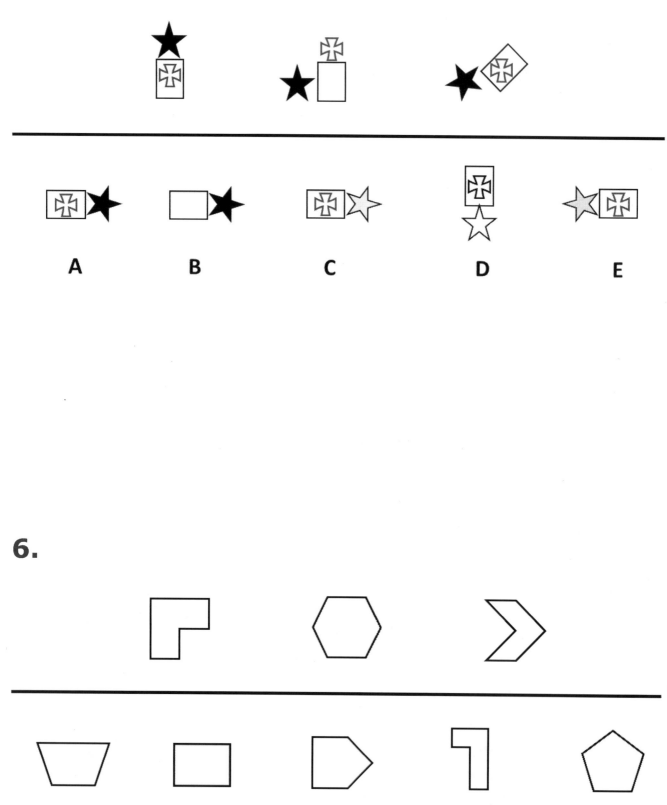

A   B   C   D   E

6.

A   B   C   D   E

7.

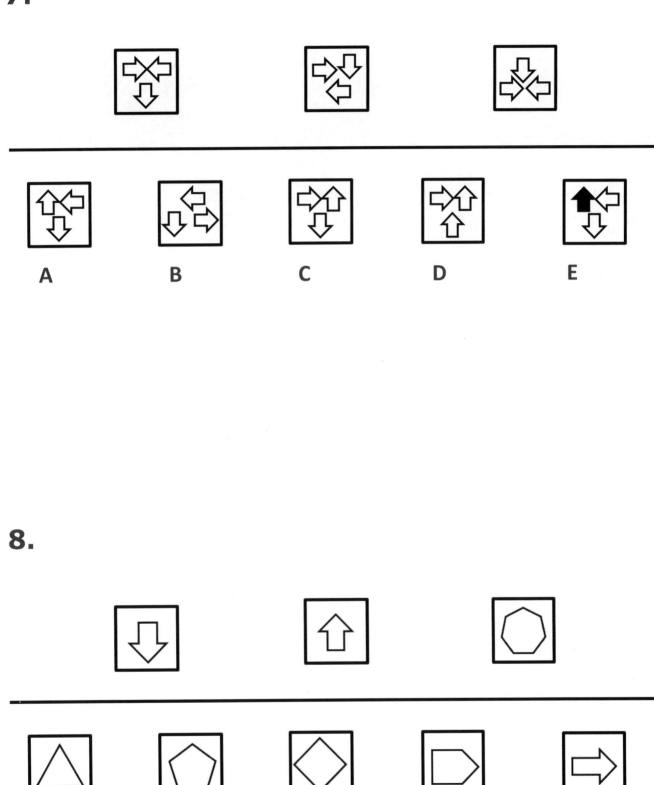

9.

A   **B**   **C**   **D**   **E**

10.

A   **B**   **C**   **D**   **E**

11.

A   **B**   **C**   **D**   **E**

12.

A   **B**   **C**   **D**   **E**

13.

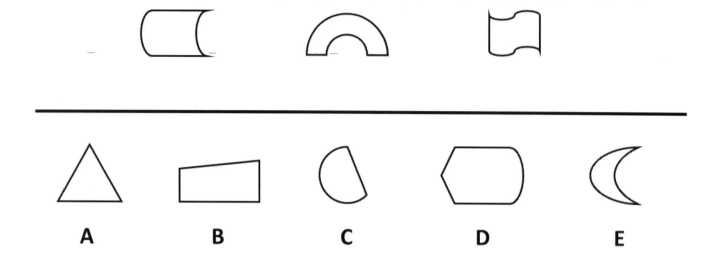

A   B   C   D   E

14.

A   B   C   D   E

15.

  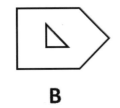

A   **B**   **C**   **D**   **E**

16.

A   **B**   **C**   **D**   **E**

17.

  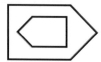

 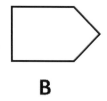

A   **B**   **C**   **D**   **E**

18.

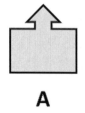  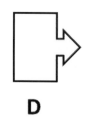

A   **B**   **C**   **D**   **E**

19.

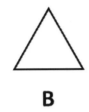 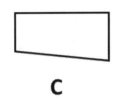 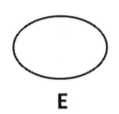

A   B   C   D   E

20.

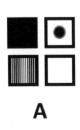   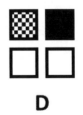 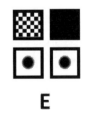

A   B   C   D   E

21.

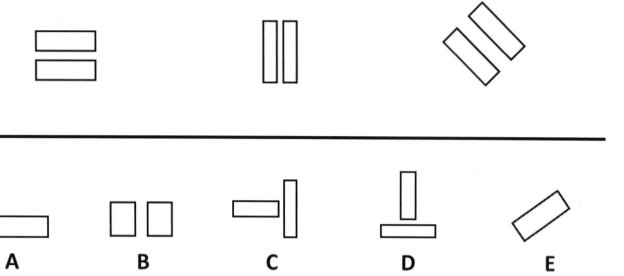

22.

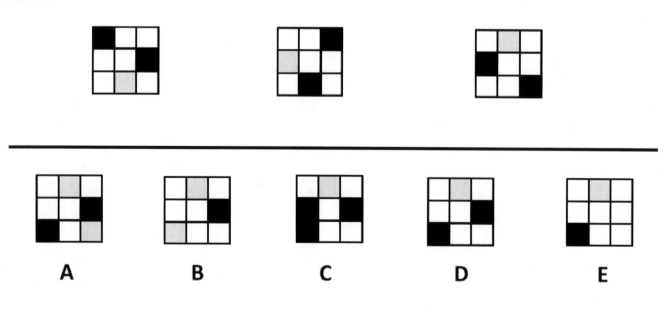

Paper Folding

Students need to determine the appearance of a perforated and folded sheet of paper, once opened.

Example

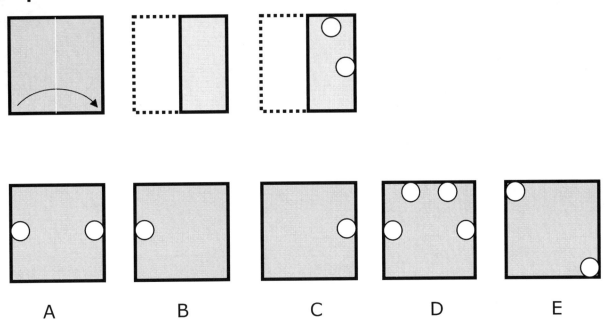

| A | B | C | D | E |

The figures at the top represent a square piece of paper being folded, and the last of these figures has two holes on it.

One of the lower five figures shows where the perforations will be when the paper is fully unfolded. You have to understand which of these images is the right one.

First, the paper was folded horizontally, from left to right.

Then, two holes were punched out. Therefore, when the paper is unfolded the holes will mirror on the left and right side of the sheet. The right answer is "D".

Tips for Paper Folding

The best way to get ready for these challenging questions is to practice. The patterns that show up on the test can confuse students, so the demonstration of folding and unfolding real paper can be very helpful.

1.

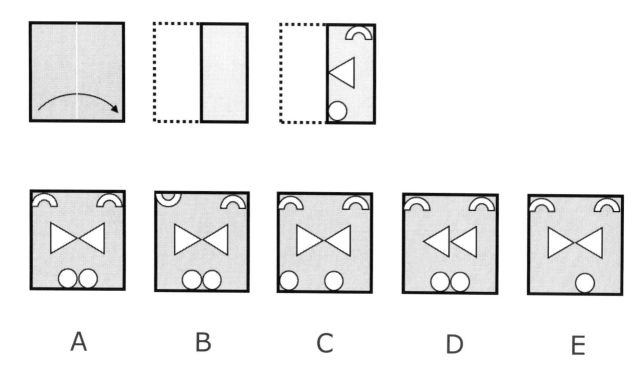

A B C D E

2.

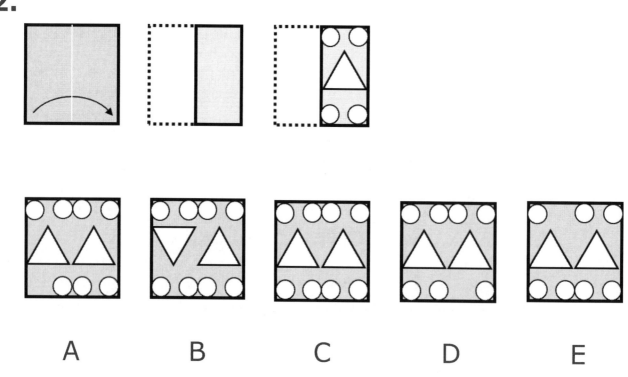

A B C D E

3.

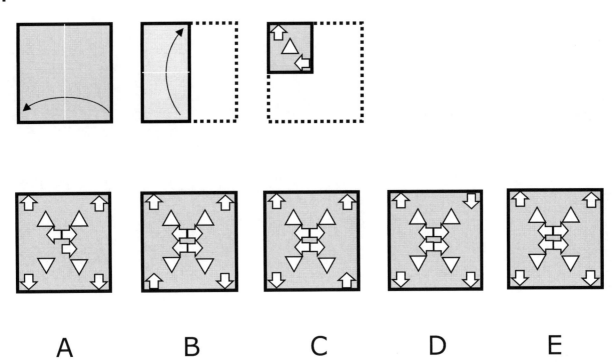

A   B   C   D   E

4.

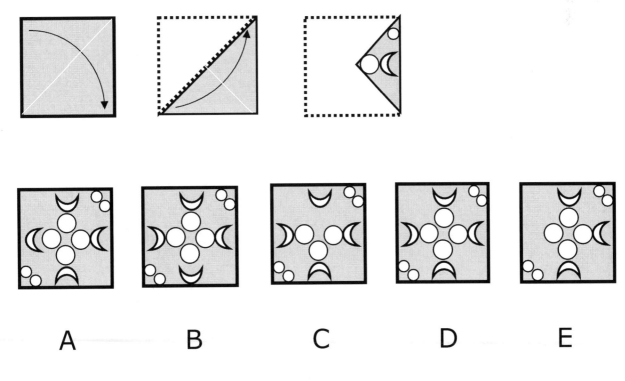

A   B   C   D   E

5.

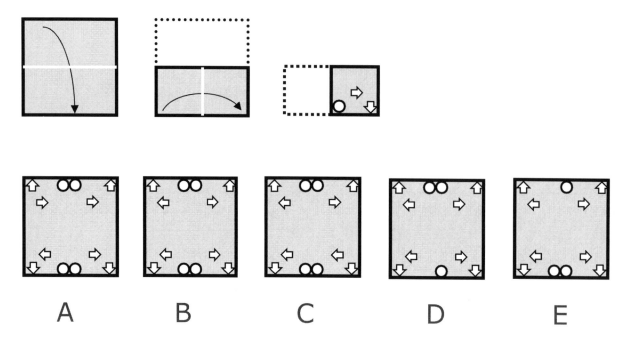

6.

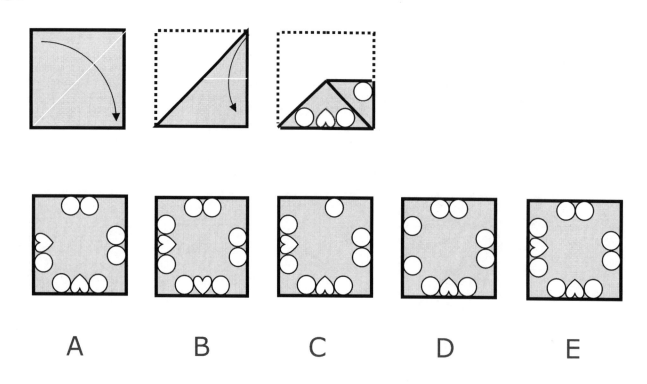

7.

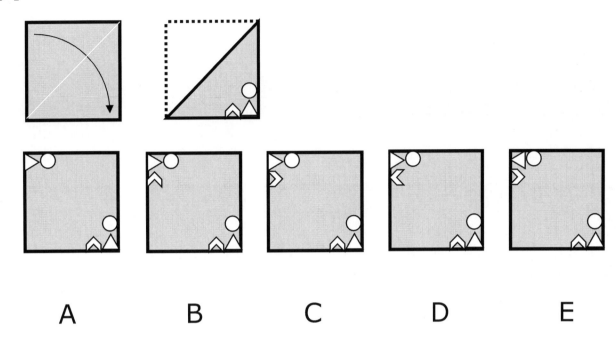

A   B   C   D   E

8.

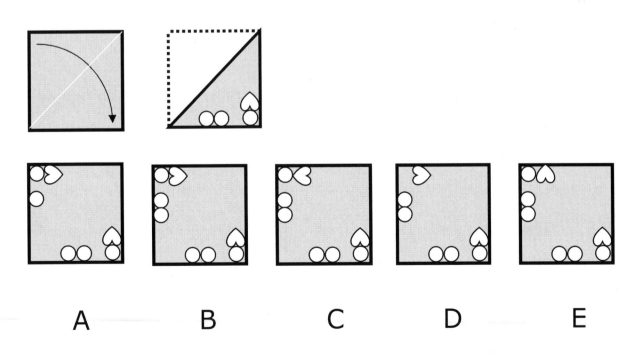

A   B   C   D   E

9.

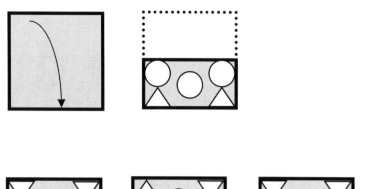

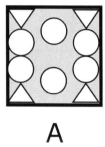 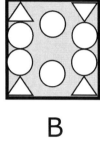  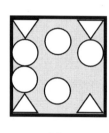 

A   B   C   D   E

10.

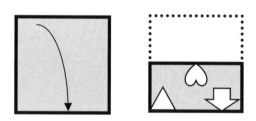

A   B   C   D   E

11.

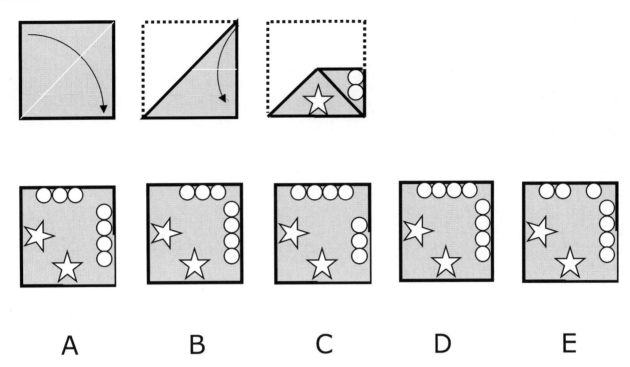

A   B   C   D   E

12.

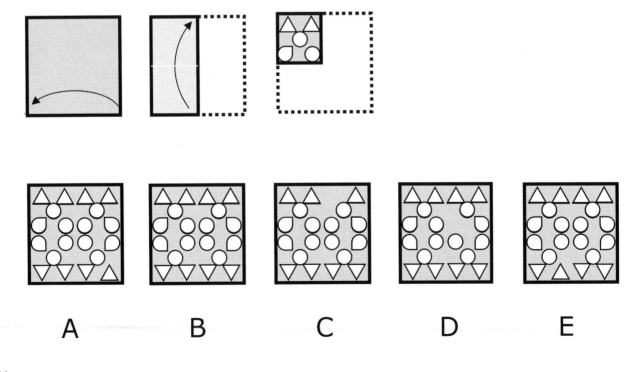

A   B   C   D   E

13.

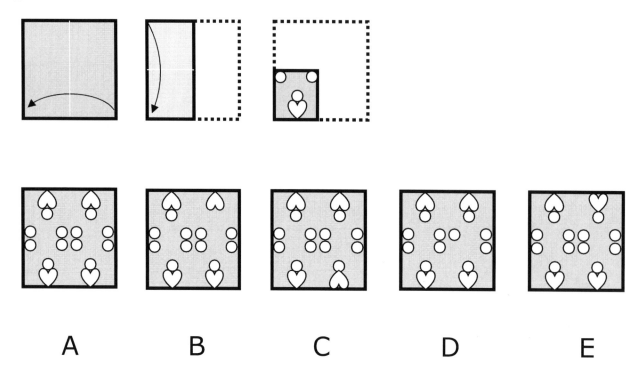

A   B   C   D   E

14.

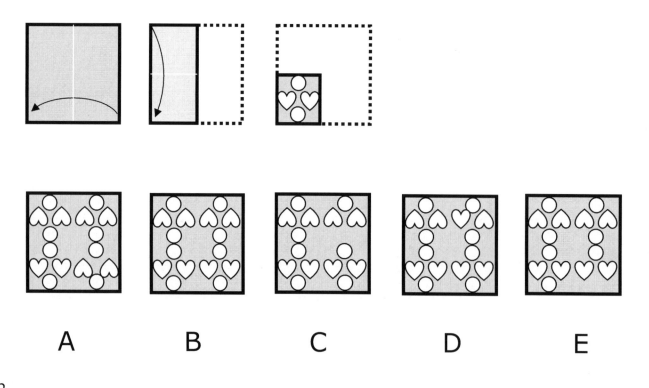

A   B   C   D   E

15.

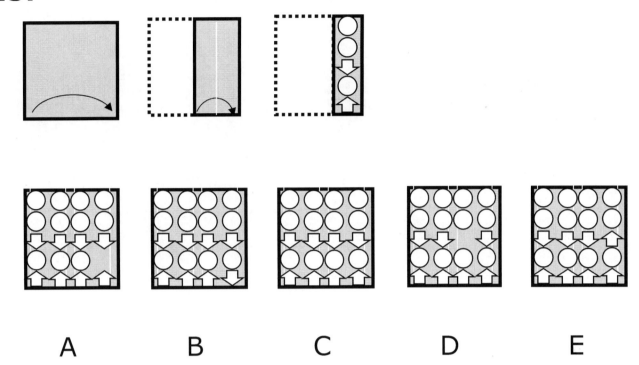

A   B   C   D   E

16.

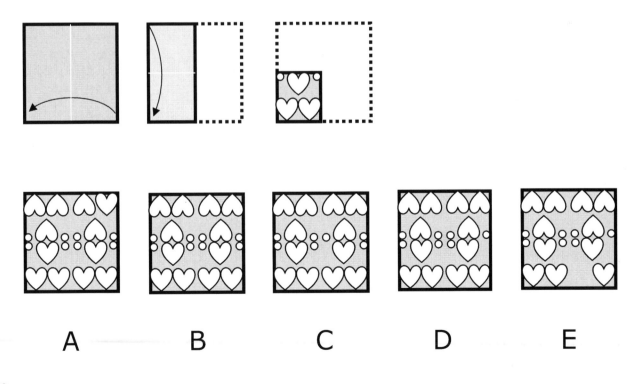

A   B   C   D   E

PRACTICE TEST 1 QUANTITATIVE BATTERY

This section introduces abstract reasoning and problem-solving skills to learners and is one of the most challenging sections in the test.

Number Puzzle

Students are required to solve basic mathematical equations. An equation says that two things are equal. It will have an equals sign "=" like this:

$$9 + 2 = 15 - 4$$

The equation says that what is on the left (9 + 2) is equal to what is on the right (15 − 4).

Example 1

$$? - 12 = 4$$

A 12   B 16   C 6   D 9   E 11

- The right side of the equal sign is 4. Which answer should be given in place of the question mark, so that the left side of the equal is also 4?

$$16 - 12 = 4; 4=4$$

The right answer is "B".

Example 2

$$? + \blacklozenge = 13$$

$$\blacklozenge = 8$$

A 3   **B** 12   **C** 5   **D** 6   **E** 8

? + 8= 13; 5+8=13; 13=13; the right answer is "C".

Tips for Number Puzzle

- Deeply understand the meaning of "equal", as the purpose is to provide the missing information that will make the two parts of the equation the same.
- Train yourself to solve simple basic equations.
- Practice with numbers and problem solving.

1.

$$? - 6 = 17$$

A 23   **B** 12   **C** 10   **D** 1   **E** 19

2.

$$? + \blacklozenge = 22$$

$$\blacklozenge = 11$$

A 13   **B** 11   **C** 15   **D** 17   **E** 10

3.

$$? + 16 = \blacklozenge$$

$$\blacklozenge = 29$$

A 10   **B** 11   **C** 13   **D** 2   **E** 21

4.

$$? \times 8 = \blacklozenge + 68$$

$$\blacklozenge = 4$$

A 13   **B** 9   **C** 14   **D** 13   **E** 18

5.

$$? - 6 = \blacklozenge + 3$$

$$\blacklozenge = 87$$

A 96   **B** 10   **C** 66   **D** 90   **E** 102

6.

$$12 + 4 = 27 - ?$$

A 22   **B** 13   **C** 11   **D** 9   **E** 5

7.

$$29 = 58 - 12 - ?$$

A 13   **B** 26   **C** 22   **D** 17   **E** 11

8.

$$17 = 38 - 21 + ?$$

A 0   **B** 5   **C** 8   **D** 11   **E** 3

9

$$61 = 11 + 21 + ?$$

A 30   **B** 31   **C** 25   **D** 30   **E** 29

10.

$$102 - 25 = 99 - ?$$

A 15   **B** 21   **C** 22   **D** 39   **E** 19

11.

$$15 + 31 = 51 - ?$$

A 12   **B** 1   **C** 26   **D** 5   **E** 81

12.

$$79 - 15 = 105 - ?$$

A 41   **B** 35   **C** 21   **D** 3   **E** 17

13.

$$? = \blacklozenge + 15$$

$$\blacklozenge = 34$$

A 53   **B** 49   **C** 6   **D** 66   **E** 22

14.

$$? = \blacklozenge \times 9$$

$$\blacklozenge = 9$$

A 60   **B** 0   **C** 77   **D** 15   **E** 81

15.

$$? \ = \ \blacklozenge \ \text{X} \ 6$$

$$\blacklozenge \ = \ 5$$

A 19   **B** 1   **C** 30   **D** 20   **E** 11

16.

$$? \ = \ \blacklozenge \ + \ 11$$

$$11 \ = \ \blacklozenge \ - \ \bullet$$

$$\bullet \ = \ 9$$

A 11   **B** 31   **C** 16   **D** 2   **E** 11

Number Analogies

In this session, you will see two pairs of numbers and then a number without its pair. The first two pairs of numbers are correlated in some way. Try to find out the correlation between the numbers within each of the pairs. Choose an answer that gives you the third pair of numbers, related to each other in the same way.

Example

[10 → 5]   [12 → 6]   [30 → ?]

A 20   **B** 1   **C** 15   **D** 7   **E** 9

- In the first two sets, you have 10 and 5; 12 and 6. Both numbers (10 and 12), are divided by 2 (10:2=5; 12:2=6).
- Apply the same rule to the number 30.

30 : 2 = 15. The right answer is "C".

Tips for Number Analogies

- Step 1: acquire all the information from the two given pairs (relationships, sums, subtractions, etc.).
- Step 2: apply the same rules, relations, formulas that you correctly identified in step 1.
- Step 3: double-check that the rule has been properly applied.

1.

[7 → 13]   [6 → 12]   [15 → ?]

A 12   **B** 21   **C** 16   **D** 1   **E** 13

2.

[6 → 18]   [5 → 15]   [11 → ?]

A 33   **B** 31   **C** 28   **D** 39   **E** 25

3.

[16 → 11]   [9 → 4]   [99 → ?]

A 88   **B** 94   **C** 81   **D** 85   **E** 61

4.

[36 → 9]   [20 → 5]   [28 → ?]

A 14   **B** 1   **C** 18   **D** 7   **E** 2

5.

[3 ⟶ 6]   [2 ⟶ 3]   [10 ⟶ ?]

A 21   **B** 17   **C** 38   **D** 25   **E** 27

6.

[2 ⟶ 24]   [3 ⟶ 36]   [6 ⟶ ?]

A 72   **B** 75   **C** 31   **D** 11   **E** 71

7.

[6 ⟶ 24]   [7 ⟶ 28]   [11 ⟶ ?]

A 41   **B** 43   **C** 44   **D** 11   **E** 29

8.

[90 ⟶ 79]   [29 ⟶ 18]   [15 ⟶ ?]

A 11   **B** 20   **C** 15   **D** 4   **E** 10

9.

[27 → 3]   [54 → 6]   [72 → ?]

A 8   **B** 13   **C** 33   **D** 1   **E** 2

10.

[15 → 22]   [29 → 36]   [11 → ?]

A 19   **B** 11   **C** 13   **D** 15   **E** 18

11.

[21 → 3]   [42 → 6]   [21 → ?]

A 10   **B** 2   **C** 3   **D** 5   **E** 90

12.

[9 → 45]   [12 → 60]   [11 → ?]

A 55   **B** 56   **C** 45   **D** 30   **E** 18

13.

[72 → 6]   [48 → 4]   [96 → ?]

A 2   **B** 4   **C** 6   **D** 8   **E** 11

14.

[19 → 6]   [25 → 12]   [31 → ?]

A 20   **B** 40   **C** 18   **D** 10   **E** 19

15.

[22 → 14]   [29 → 21]   [49 → ?]

A 18   **B** 41   **C** 12   **D** 56   **E** 11

16.

[15 → 225]   [5 → 75]   [4 → ?]

A 11   **B** 13   **C** 45   **D** 60   **E** 68

17.

[68 → 17]   [12 → 3]   [84 → ?]

A 21   **B** 18   **C** 3   **D** 15   **E** 22

18.

[7 → 31]   [4 → 16]   [2 → ?]

A 9   **B** 6   **C** 3   **D** 1   **E** 8

Number Series

Students are provided with a sequence of numbers that follow a pattern. They are required to identify which number should come next in the sequence.

Example 1

$$3 \quad 6 \quad 9 \quad 12 \quad ?$$

A 15   **B** 13   **C** 19   **D** 6   **E** 80

- It's easy to realize that each number in the sequence increases by 3. 3+3=6; 6+3=9; 9+3=12; etc.
- Apply the same rule to the number 12.

12 + 3 = 15. The right answer is "A".

Example 2

$$3 \quad 6 \quad 4 \quad 7 \quad 5 \quad ?$$

A 5   **B** 1   **C** 11   **D** 10   **E** 8

- The sequence follows the rule: +3, -2, +3, -2, +3, etc. 3+3=6; 6-2=4; 4+3=7; 7-2=5; etc.
- Apply the same rule to the number 5.

5 + 3 = 8 The right answer is "E".

Tips for Number Series

- To correctly answer these questions, the student will need to be able to identify the patterns in a sequence of numbers and provide the missing item. Therefore, it is important to practice, working with sequences of numbers.

1.

    8   **11**   **14**   **17**   **?**

A 20   **B** 21   **C** 22   **D** 90   **E** 12

2.

    25   **21**   **17**   **13**   **9**   **?**

A 10   **B** 11   **C** 5   **D** 17   **E** 18

3.

    6   **3**   **5**   **2**   **4**   **?**

A 4   **B** 8   **C** 39   **D** 9   **E** 1

4.

    16 **20** **17** **21** **18** **22** **19** **?**

A 31   **B** 23   **C** 25   **D** 12   **E** 19

5.

14   **17**   **21**   **26**   **?**

A 25   **B** 11   **C** 28   **D** 31   **E** 32

6.

3   **0**   **12**   **9**   **21**   **18**   **?**

A 28   **B** 35   **C** 30   **D** 21   **E** 33

7.

9   **0**   **9**   **0**   **9**   **?**

A 0   **B** 12   **C** 4   **D** 7   **E** 8

8.

18   **13**   **15**   **10**   **12**   **7**   **?**

A 5   **B** 8   **C** 9   **D** 6   **E** 12

9.

| 70 | 61 | 52 | 43 | 34 | ? |

A 25   **B** 30   **C** 12   **D** 35   **E** 39

10.

| 1 | 7 | 10 | 16 | 19 | 25 | ? |

A 8   **B** 21   **C** 20   **D** 1   **E** 28

11.

| 2 | 10 | 8 | 16 | 14 | 22 | ? |

A 13   **B** 20   **C** 16   **D** 19   **E** 91

12.

| 3 | 16 | 29 | 42 | 55 | 68 | ? |

A 71   **B** 81   **C** 56   **D** 23   **E** 32

13.

5   12   9   16   13   20   ?

A 6   **B** 11   **C** 21   **D** 30   **E** 17

14.

0.1   2.1   4.1   6.1   8.1   10.1   ?

A 5.1   **B** 12.1   **C** 7   **D** 3.3   **E** 8.3

15.

0.03   0.07   0.11   0.15   0.19   ?

A 0.02   **B** 0.24   **C** 0.3   **D** 0.23   **E** 0.6

16.

97   91   85   79   73   67   ?

A 61   **B** 68   **C** 66   **D** 36   **E** 35

17.

6.5   7.1   7.7   8.3   8.9   9.5   ?

A 9.8   **B** 6.5   **C** 10.1   **D** 10.2   **E** 5.2

18.

8   7.98   7.96   7.94   7.92   7,90   ?

A 7.88   **B** 3.8   **C** 7.56   **D** 7.22   **E** 7.3

ANSWER KEY TEST 1

Verbal Analogies Practice Test
p.13

1.
Answer: option B
Explanation: gold is a metal; hydrogen is a gas.

2.
Answer: option C
Explanation: four is a number; inch is a unit of length.

3.
Answer: option D
Explanation: the minute is divided into seconds; the day is divided into hours.

4.
Answer: option B
Explanation: the degree Celsius is a unit of temperature; the gram is a unit of weight.

5.
Answer: option A
Explanation: the teeth are for chewing; the nose is for sniffing.

6.
Answer: option C
Explanation: cm is the abbreviation of centimeter; mm is the abbreviation of millimeter.

7.
Answer: option D
Explanation: sour is the taste of a lemon; sweet is the taste of a candy.

8.
Answer: option A
Explanation: "flow" describes the movement of water; "billow" describes the movement of smoke.

9.
Answer: option B
Explanation: an arc is a part of a circle; a line segment is a part of a line.

10.
Answer: option C
Explanation: synonyms

11.
Answer: option B
Explanation: antonyms.

12.
Answer: option D
Explanation: fog and hail are both varieties of weather; yellow and red are both varieties of colors.

13.
Answer: option B
Explanation: a window is a part of a wall; an engine is a part of a plane.

14.
Answer: option E
Explanation: an apple is an example of a fruit; Jupiter is an example of a planet.

15.
Answer: option E
Explanation: humans are vertebrates; worms are invertebrates.

16.
Answer: option C
Explanation: Nigeria is in Africa; Germany is in Europe.

17.
Answer: option C
Explanation: corn is found in the cob; peas are found in the pod.

18.
Answer: option A
Explanation: antonyms.

19.
Answer: option A
Explanation: eyes allow us to see; feet allow us to walk.

20.
Answer: option D
Explanation: the pedal is a part of the bicycle; the hard drive is a part of the computer.

21.
Answer: option B
Explanation: giraffe is a mammal; spider is an arachnid.

22.
Answer: option B
Explanation: a engine is a part of a car; a tree is a part of a forest.

23.
Answer: option E
Explanation: the first word is an impairment of the second word.

24.
Answer: option C
Explanation: antonyms.

Verbal Classification Practice Test
p.20

1.
Answer: option C
Explanation: constitutional, congregational, constructivism, congratulation are words that start with "con".

2.
Answer: option B
Explanation: democracy, oligarchy, dictatorship, and monarchy are types of government.

3.
Answer: option C
Explanation: acute, right, obtuse, and straight are types of angles.

4.
Answer: option A
Explanation: Aries, Taurus, Gemini, and Virgo are types of zodiac signs.

5.
Answer: option C
Explanation: alexandrite, amber, zircon, and turquoise are types of gemstones.

6.
Answer: option E
Explanation: non-verbal, verbal, written, and visual are types of communication styles.

7.
Answer: option A
Explanation: hydrogen, fluorine, helium, and neon are types of gas elements.

8.
Answer: option D
Explanation: gravitational, chemical, radiant, and elastic are types of energy.

9.
Answer: option D
Explanation: natural, whole, rational, and real are types of numbers.

10.
Answer: option A
Explanation: duodenum, appendix, colon, and rectum are parts of intestine.

11.
Answer: option E
Explanation: Bronx, Brooklyn, Manhattan, and Staten Island are boroughs of New York

12.
Answer: option A
Explanation: Icelandic, Strombolian, Plinian, and Hawaiian are types of volcanic eruption.

13.
Answer: option A
Explanation: hurricane, tornadoes, tsunamis, and thunderstorms are categories of natural disasters

14.
Answer: option C
Explanation: maroon, scarlet, crimson, and cerise are types of red.

15.
Answer: option C
Explanation: almonds, hazelnuts, pecans, and pistachios are types of nuts.

16.
Answer: option A
Explanation: said, got, took, and saw are past tense verbs.

17.
Answer: option D
Explanation: carbohydrates, proteins, fats and vitamins are nutrients in food.

18.
Answer: option B
Explanation: rectangles, rhombus, squares, and trapezoids have at least 2 parallel sides

19.
Answer: option E
Explanation: Zebra Longwing, Ulysses, Blue Clipper, and Monarch are types of butterflies.

20.
Answer: option A
Explanation: tractors, seeders, balers, and plows are farm-specific vehicles.

Sentence Completion Practice Test
p.26

1.
Answer: option E
Explanation: electronic resource= a resource that requires computer access.

2.
Answer: option A
Explanation: changing= facing a different direction.

3.
Answer: option B
Explanation: different= not the same.

4.
Answer: option C
Explanation: mark = make a visible impression.

5.
Answer: option C
Explanation: worse= more unfavorable, difficult, unpleasant, or painful.

6.
Answer: option D
Explanation: symbol= a thing that represents or stands for something else.

7.
Answer: option E
Explanation: chemical= a substance that is produced or used in a process involving changes to atoms or molecules.

8.
Answer: option A
Explanation: maintain = to keep in an existing state.

9.
Answer: option B
Explanation: visible= capable of being seen.

10.
Answer: option B
Explanation: follow= come after.

11.
Answer: option E
Explanation: through = from one side to the other.

12.
Answer: option A
Explanation: harsh= severe and unpleasant:

13.
Answer: option D
Explanation: change = became different.

14.
Answer: option C
Explanation: pure= not mixed or adulterated with any other substance or material.

15.
Answer: option A
Explanation: shape= appearance.

16.
Answer: option D
Explanation: economy = production and consumption of goods and services and the supply of money.

17.
Answer: option B
Explanation: short=brief.

18.
Answer: option B
Explanation: body = the physical structure, including the bones, flesh, and organs, of a person or an animal.

19.
Answer: option D
Explanation: prosthetic = denoting an artificial body part.

20.
Answer: option B
Explanation: draw = trace.

Figure Matrices Practice Test
p.35

1.
Answer: option B
Explanation: the figure is rotated by 90 degrees counterclockwise. The white circle turns black.

2.
Answer: option A
Explanation: the white figure is flipped vertically and becomes black.

3.
Answer: option B
Explanation: the bottom left element turns gray; the bottom right element turns white.

4.
Answer: option A
Explanation: the internal figure becomes external and vice versa.

5.
Answer: option E
Explanation: the figures get separated and the one on the right turns black.

6.
Answer: option C
Explanation: one side of the triangle is removed and a black heart is added.

7.
Answer: option B
Explanation: the figure is rotated by 90 degrees clockwise.

8.
Answer: option D
Explanation: the outer figure disappears; the inner figure doubles.

9.
Answer: option A
Explanation: the bottom figure moves up and is flipped vertically.

10.
Answer: option E
Explanation: the larger figure turns gray; the black circle moves up.

11.
Answer: option D
Explanation: the figure rotates 45 degrees clockwise and turns gray.

12.
Answer: option C
Explanation: the figure rotates by 180 degrees clockwise and turns gray. The black dot is removed.

13.
Answer: option A
Explanation: 90-degree rotation counterclockwise.

14.
Answer: option B
Explanation: the figure is flipped vertically and turns gray. A black arrow is removed.

15.
Answer: option D
Explanation: the inside figure is flipped vertically and becomes black; the larger figure becomes gray.

16.
Answer: option A
Explanation: the white star turns gray; the white circle turns black.

17.
Answer: option C
Explanation: addition of a white circle over the figures on the left.

18.
Answer: option B
Explanation: the figure is composed of 2 shapes; the shape on the left is flipped vertically and becomes black; the shape on the right does not change.

19.
Answer: option E
Explanation: the figure is composed of 2 shapes; the bottom shape is flipped vertically; the top shape rotates by 90 degrees clockwise and becomes gray.

20.
Answer: option C
Explanation: the figure rotates by 45 degrees clockwise and does not change color.

21.
Answer: option B
Explanation: the larger figure turns black; the smaller figure moves to the left.

22.
Answer: option D
Explanation: the outer figure rotates 90 degrees clockwise; the inside triangle turns black

Figure Classification Practice Test
p.44

1.
Answer: option A
Explanation: same figure, rotated.

2.
Answer: option E
Explanation: in each figure, there are 3 black parts and 5 white parts.

3.
Answer: option D
Explanation: the number of black circles is equal to the number of white circles.

4.
Answer: option B
Explanation: same figure rotated, same colors.

5.
Answer: option A
Explanation: combos of a white rectangle, a black star and a white cross.

6.
Answer: option D
Explanation: 6-sided figures

7.

Answer: option B

Explanation: in each square, there are 3 arrows, one pointing right, one pointing left, and one pointing down.

8.

Answer: option E

Explanation: each square contains a 7-sided figure.

9.

Answer: option D

Explanation: black figures.

10.

Answer: option C

Explanation: combos of 2 white arrows, a grey heart and a black heart.

11.

Answer: option D

Explanation: combos of a white arrow pointing up, a white arrow pointing down, a gray arrow pointing right, a black arrow pointing left.

12.

Answer: option A

Explanation: combos of a white circle and two white hearts pointing down.

13.

Answer: option E

Explanation: all figures have 2 non-linear sides.

14.

Answer: option A

Explanation: all figures have the same kind of shapes inside, but rotated 90 degrees clockwise.

15.
Answer: option E
Explanation: the internal and external figures have the same number of sides.

16.
Answer: option B
Explanation: combos of a white star, five black circles and a white circle.

17.
Answer: option C
Explanation: the inside arrow is flipped horizontally compared to the larger arrow.

18.
Answer: option A
Explanation: same grey figure, rotated.

19.
Answer: option C
Explanation: all figures have only one oblique side.

20.
Answer: option C
Explanation: same rotated figure composed of 4 squares in different colors and a black circle inside a square.

21.
Answer: option B
Explanation: 2 parallel elements.

22.
Answer: option D
Explanation: same rotated figure, consisting of 6 white squares, a gray square and two black squares.

Paper Folding Practice Test

p.56

1.
Answer: option A

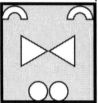

2.
Answer: option C

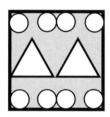

3.
Answer: option E

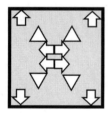

4.
Answer: option D

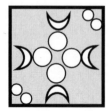

5.
Answer: option B

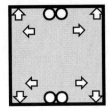

6.
Answer: option E

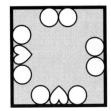

7
Answer: option C

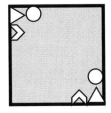

8.
Answer: option B

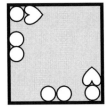

9.
Answer: option A

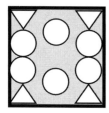

10.
Answer: option B

11.
Answer: option D

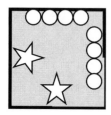

12.
Answer: option B

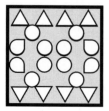

13.
Answer: option A

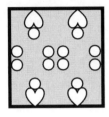

14.
Answer: option B

15.
Answer: option C

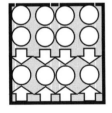

16.
Answer: option B

Number Puzzle Practice Test
p.67

1.
Answer: option A
Explanation: 23-6=17; 17=17

2.
Answer: option B
Explanation: 11+11=22; 22=22

3.
Answer: option C
Explanation: 13+16=29; 29=29

4.
Answer: option B
Explanation: 9X8=4+68; 72=72

5.
Answer: option A
Explanation: 96-6=87+3; 90=90

6.
Answer: option C
Explanation: 12+4=27-11; 16=16

7.
Answer: option D
Explanation: 29=58-12-17; 29=29

8.
Answer: option A
Explanation: 17=38-21+0; 17=17

9.
Answer: option E
Explanation: 61=11+21+29; 61=11+50; 61=61

10.
Answer: option C
Explanation: 102-25=99 -22; 77=77

11.
Answer: option D
Explanation: 15+31=51-5; 46=46

12.
Answer: option A
Explanation: 79-15 =105-41; 64=64

13.
Answer: option B
Explanation: 49=34+15; 49=49

14.
Answer: option E
Explanation: 81=9X9; 81=81

15.
Answer: option C
Explanation: 30=5X6; 30=30

16.
Answer: option B
Explanation: 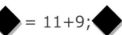 = 11+9; ◆ =20; 31=20+11; 31=31

Number Analogies Practice Test
p.73

1.
Answer: option B
Explanation: 7+6=13   6+6=12   15+6=21

2.
Answer: option A
Explanation: 6X3=18   5X3=15   11X3=33

3.
Answer: option B
Explanation: 16-5=11   9-5=4   99-5=94

4.
Answer: option D
Explanation: 36:4=9   20:4=5   28:4=7

5.
Answer: option E
Explanation: 3X3=9; 9-3=6   2X3=6; 6-3=3   10X3=30; 30-3=27

6.
Answer: option A
Explanation: 2X12=24   3X12=36   6X12=72

7.
Answer: option C
Explanation: 6X4=24; 7X4=28; 11X4=44;

8.
Answer: option D
Explanation: 90-11=79   29-11=18   15-11=4

9.
Answer: option A
Explanation: 27:9=3   54:9=6   72:9=8

10.
Answer: option E
Explanation: 15+7=22   29+7=36   11+7=18

11.
Answer: option C
Explanation: 21:7=3   42:7=6   21:7=3

12.
Answer: option A
Explanation: 9X5=45   12X5=60   11X5=55

13.
Answer: option D
Explanation: 72:12=6   48:12=4   96:12=8

14.
Answer: option C
Explanation: 19-13=6   25-13=12   31-13=18

15.
Answer: option B
Explanation: 22-8=14   29-8=21   49-8=41

16.
Answer: option D
Explanation: 15X15=225   5X15=75   4X15=60

17.
Answer: option A
Explanation: 68:4=17   12:4=3   84:4=21

18.
Answer: option B
Explanation: 7X5=35; 35-4=31   4X5=20; 20-4=16
2X5=10; 10-4=6

Number Series Practice Test
p.79

1.
Answer: option A
Explanation: +3, +3, +3, +3, etc. 8+3=11; 11+3=14; 14+3=17; 17+3=20

2.
Answer: option C
Explanation: -4, -4, -4, -4, -4, etc.

3.
Answer: option E
Explanation: -3, +2, -3, +2, -3

4.
Answer: option B
Explanation: +4, -3, +4, -3, +4, -3, +4, etc.

5.
Answer: option E
Explanation: +3, +4, +5, +6, etc.

6.
Answer: option C
Explanation: -3, +12, -3, +12, -3, +12, etc.

7.
Answer: option A
Explanation: -9, +9, -9, +9, -9, etc.

8.
Answer: option C
Explanation: -5, +2, -5, +2, -5, +2, etc.

9.
Answer: option A
Explanation: -9, -9, -9, -9, -9, etc.

10.
Answer: option E
Explanation: +6, +3, +6, +3, +6, +3, etc.

11.
Answer: option B
Explanation: +8, -2, +8, -2, +8, -2, etc.

12.
Answer: option B
Explanation: +13, +13, +13, +13, +13, +13, etc.

13.
Answer: option E
Explanation: +7, -3, +7, -3, +7, -3, etc.

14.
Answer: option B
Explanation: +2, +2, +2, +2, +2, +2, etc.

15.
Answer: option D
Explanation: +0.04, +0.04, +0.04, +0.04, +0.04, +0.04, etc.

16.
Answer: option A
Explanation: -6, -6, -6, -6, -6, -6, etc.

17.
Answer: option C
Explanation: +0.6, +0.6, +0.6, +0.6, +0.6, +0.6, etc.

18.
Answer: option A
Explanation: -0.02, -0.02, -0.02, -0.02, -0.02, -0.02, etc.

PRACTICE TEST 2 VERBAL BATTERY

Verbal Analogies

1.

pentagon → five : dodecagon →

A two   **B** twelve   **C** seven   **D** ten
E twenty

2.

centimeter→ ce: weight →

A we   **B** ht   **C** centimeter   **D** er   **E** kg

3.

admit → confess: connect →

A chop   **B** divide   **C** join   **D** part   **E** know

4.

denim → cotton : linen →

A paper   **B** metal   **C** gas   **D** flax   **E** rock

5.

guilty ⟶ innocent : abundance ⟶

A full   **B** lack   **C** wealth   **D** health   **E** sadness

6.

seraphim ⟶ angel: nymph ⟶

A mermaid   **B** witch   **C** devil   **D** river   **E** maiden

7.

tree ⟶ ree : table ⟶

A wood   **B** able   **C** fire   **D** sable   **E** chair

8.

segregate ⟶ unify : repair ⟶

A cure   **B** gather   **C** sink   **D** adjust   **E** damage

9.

opossum → marsupial : seal →

A fish   **B** primate   **C** mammal   **D** reptile
E amphibian

10.

cicada → insect: fox →

A canine   **B** animal   **C** reptile   **D** bear
E wolf

11.

geology → rocks: ornithology →

A snakes   **B** birds   **C** bears   **D** bats   **E** cats

12.

purse → money : urn →

A sand   **B** rain   **C** snow   **D** ashes   **E** dust

13.

ribbon → present : icing →

A car   **B** table   **C** cake   **D** meat   **E** birthday

14.

whale → ocean : slug →

A land   **B** universe   **C** sky   **D** Jupiter   **E** river

15.

spoke → wheel : word →

A pen   **B** table   **C** tree   **D** sentence   **E** lamp

16.

engine → car: vamp →

A shoe   **B** tree   **C** body   **D** hair   **E** hand

17.
drive → golf : serve →

A ski **B** tennis **C** swimming **D** running **E** karate

18.
pestle → grinding : saw →

A pounding **B** weighing **C** smoothing **D** pasting
E cutting

19.
stigma → flower : atom →

A wall **B** dog **C** molecule **D** electron **E** neutron

20.
scalpel → incision : spatula →

A hole **B** lifting **C** cut **D** color **E** wrinkle

120

21.

atlas → maps : dictionary →

A definitions **B** poems **C** tales **D** recipes **E** fruits

22.

bonsai → pot : sequoia →

A prison **B** forest **C** water **D** desert **E** mud

23.

comical → pathetic : early →

A after **B** before **C** always **D** soon **E** late

24.

mechanic → garage : professor →

A hospital **B** court **C** museum **D** college
E house

Verbal Classification

1.

nucleus, neutron, proton

A cyclone   **B** hyperventilation.   **C** congratulation
D staphylococcus   **E** electron

2.

body, ability, academy

A leg   **B** hand   **C** head   **D** city   **E** museum

3.

frame, saddle, wheel

A engine   **B** pedal   **C** car   **D** leg   **E** hand

4.

crown, root, pulp

A cementum   **B** acid   **C** mouth   **D** tongue   **E** spittle

5.

stern, bow, anchor

A sail   **B** pedal   **C** branch   **D** stone   **E** pot

6.

date, closing, body

A book   **B** poem   **C** signature   **D** floor   **E** window

7.

Fuji, Gala, Golden delicious

A Andorra   **B** Rome   **C** Belgium   **D** Atlantic
E Granny Smith

8.

personal, relative, possessive

A new   **B** indefinite   **C** old   **D** elastic   **E** cold

9.
iguanodon, allosaurus, carnotaurus

A artificial   **B** acanthous   **C** acidulous
D albertosaurus   **E** abnormous

10.
akasa, bamboo, teak

A pine   **B** copper   **C** zinc   **D** plastic   **E** skin

11.
political, physical, topographic

A punctured **B** damaged **C** dirty **D** disfigured
E geologic

12.
incisors, canine, molar

A scapula   **B** premolar   **C** pelvis   **D** ulna
E radius

13.

histogram, line, bar

A snow   **B** pie   **C** strawberry   **D** cherry
E summer

14.

grenade, crossbow, sword

A torpedo   **B** table   **C** carpet   **D** toy
E umbrella

15.

imperative, declarative, exclamatory

A numerals   **B** possessive   **C** purpose
D recurring   **E** interrogative

16.

A, C, D

A Y   **B** Z   **C** K   **D** W   **E** X

17.

medulla, hypothalamus, cerebellum

A ileum   **B** appendix   **C** pancreas   **D** pituitary
gland   **E** fibula

18.

keyboard, camera, screen

A touchpad   **B** hammer   **C** muzzle   **D** roof
E seat

19.

lenses, bridge, nose pads

A condenser   **B** mirror   **C** body tube   **D** tripod
E rims

20.

clavicle, scapula, sternum

A peroneus   **B** radius   **C** shoulder   **D** leg
E aorta

Sentence Completion

1.

The squirrel disappeared into a _____ at the base of the tree.

A house **B** car **C** hollow **D** street **E** mushroom

2.

Sarah is Jane's friend but she is _____ if Jane plays with other girls.

A happy   **B** honest   **C** excited   **D** jealous
E brave

3.

John looked ridiculous in leather trousers, and I was desperately trying to keep a _____ face.

A straight **B** excited **C** old **D** strange **E** dirty

4.

In any country, the rich can invest and reinvest their capital, _____ greater and greater profits.

A destroying   **B** eliminating   **C** reducing
D producing   **E** joining

5.

I've had a stressful day at work and it's left me feeling a bit _____.

A energetic   **B** frazzled   **C** old   **D** rich
E delicious

6.

The practice is not a very lucrative one at the moment, but if it is worked up it' should prove quite _____.

A profitable   **B** ruinous   **C** new   **D** symbolic
E real

7.

Before creating this sculpture, Mary _____ all the masterpieces of classical antiquity.

A sold   **B** bought   **C** destroyed   **D** painted
E studied

8.

The area was an important resting _____ for many types of migrant birds.

A school   **B** place   **C** museum   **D** cage
E ship

9.

The seafloor around Iceland provides excellent examples of _____ volcanic structures.

A invisible   **B** nice   **C** submarine   **D** arid
E Romanic

10.

An eclipse involving the Sun, Earth, and Moon can occur only when they are nearly in a straight line, allowing one to be _____ behind another.

A seen   **B** died   **C** colored   **D** hidden   **E** lifted

11.

Fever seems to play a key role in _____ your body fight off a number of infections.

A discouraging   **B** helping   **C** refusing
D hindering   **E** hampering

12.

Adverbs are especially important for indicating the time, manner, _____, degree and frequency of something.

A color   **B** beauty   **C** place   **D** sympathy
E honesty

13.

In its most basic form, a sentence is made up of a subject and predicate, which is the verb and the words that _____.

A precede **B** start **C** follow **D** change **E** support

14.

Country is the usual word for talking about a large area of land with recognized _____ borders, like Italy, Mexico, or Japan.

A colorful **B** round **C** linear **D** useless
E political

15.

The quadrupedal Stegosaurus is one of the most easily identifiable dinosaur genera, due to the distinctive double row of kite-shaped plates rising _____ along the rounded back.

A obliquely **B** horizontally **C** vertically
D in parallel **E** circularly

16.

During the High Middle Ages, which began after 1000, the population of Europe increased greatly as technological and agricultural innovations _____ trade to flourish.

A prevent   **B** blocked   **C** arrested   **D** averted
E allowed

17.

All sheep have a tendency to congregate close to other members of a flock, and sheep can become _____ when separated from their flock members.

A happy   **B** stressed   **C** beautiful   **D** fatter
E nice

18.

The most commonly used cake ingredients include flour, sugar, eggs, butter, a liquid, and a _____ agent, such as baking soda or baking powder.

A leavening   **B** dye   **C** glue   **D** heating
E cooling

19.

Dolphins are capable of making a broad range of _____ using nasal air sacs located just below the blowhole.

A jumps   **B** breaths   **C** sounds   **D** yawns
E racing

20.

The development of affordable, inexhaustible, and _____solar energy technologies will have huge longer-term benefits.

A old   **B** clean   **C** contaminated   **D** warm
E fresh

PRACTICE TEST 2 NON VERBAL BATTERY

Figure Matrices

1.

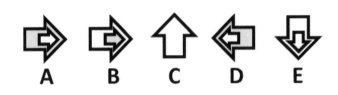

2.

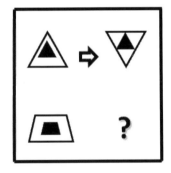

3.

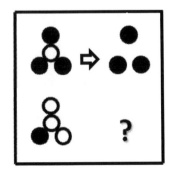
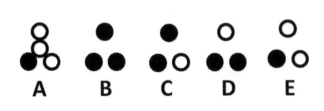

4.

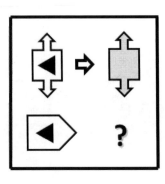

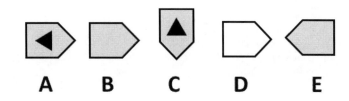

5.

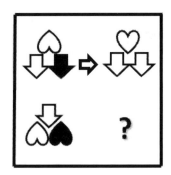

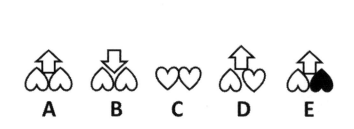

6.

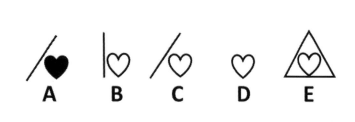

7.

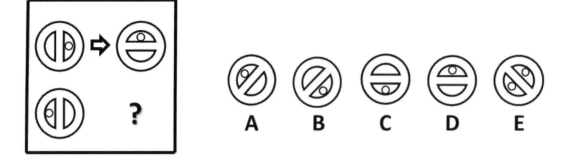

8.

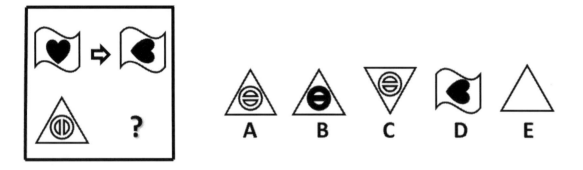

9.

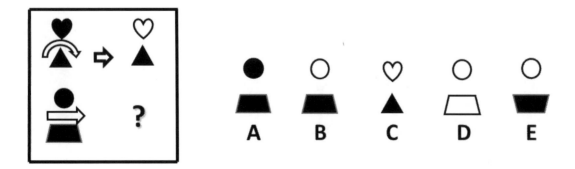

10.

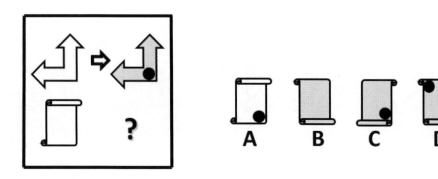

11.

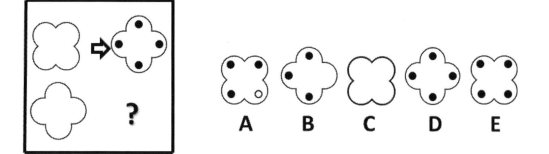

12.

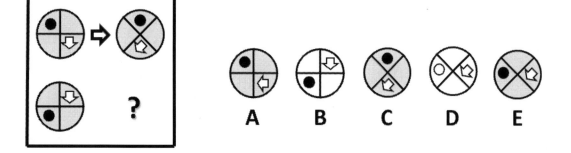

13.

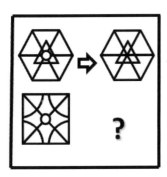

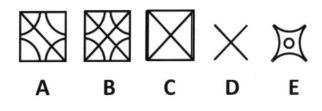

14.

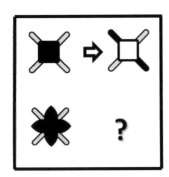

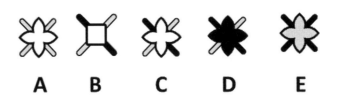

15.

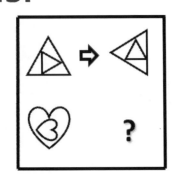

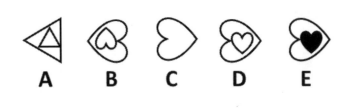

16.

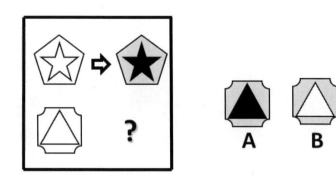

17.

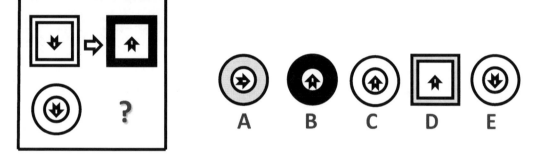

18.

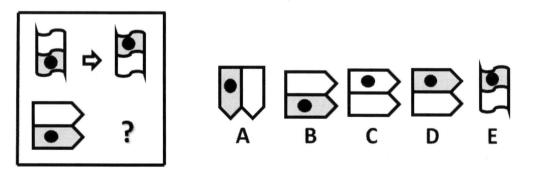

19.

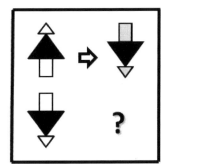

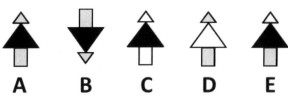

20.

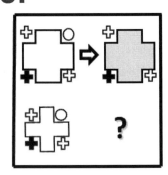

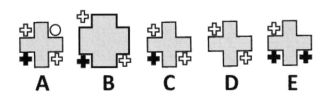

21.

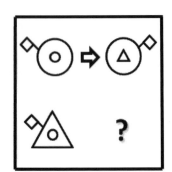

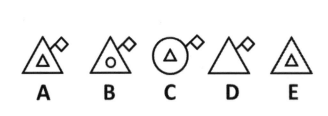

22.

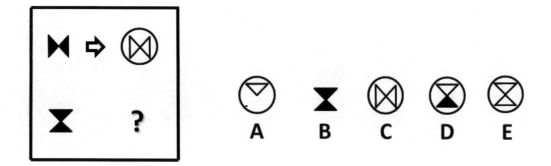

Figure Classification

1.

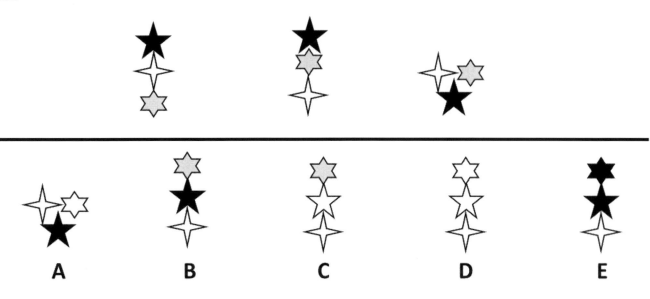

2.

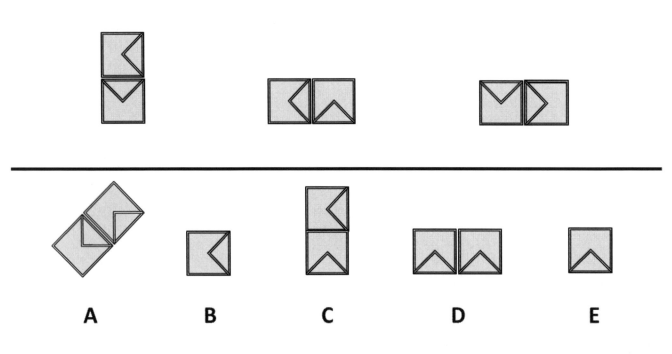

3.

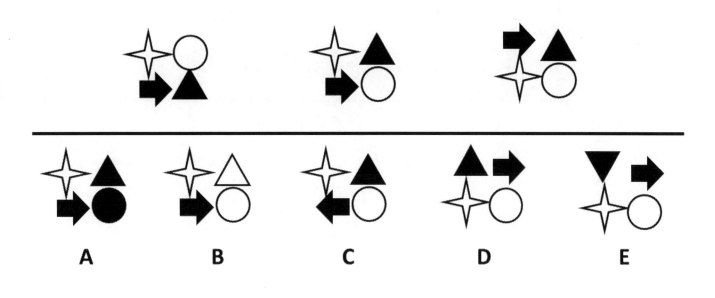

     B

A   **B**   **C**   **D**   **E**

4.

A   **B**   **C**   **D**   **E**

5.

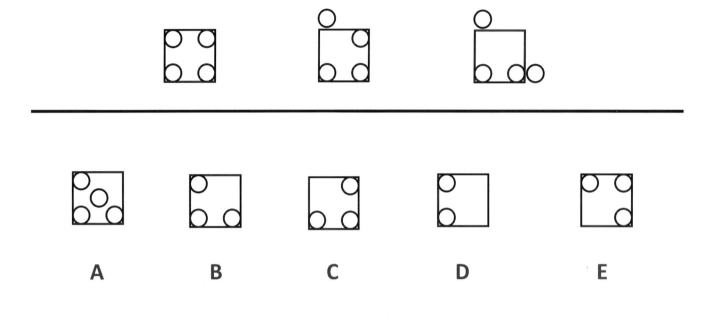

6.

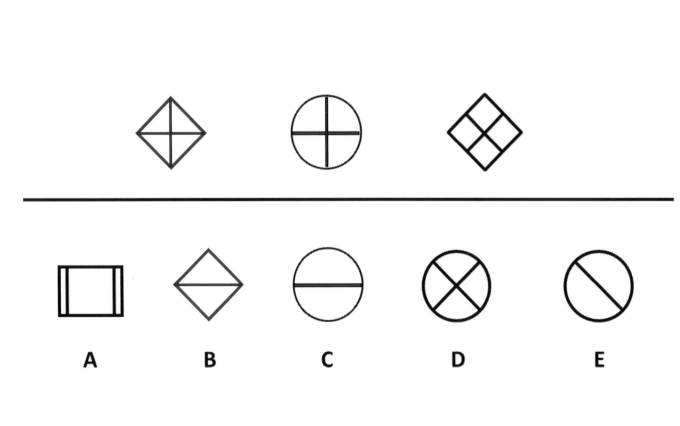

7.

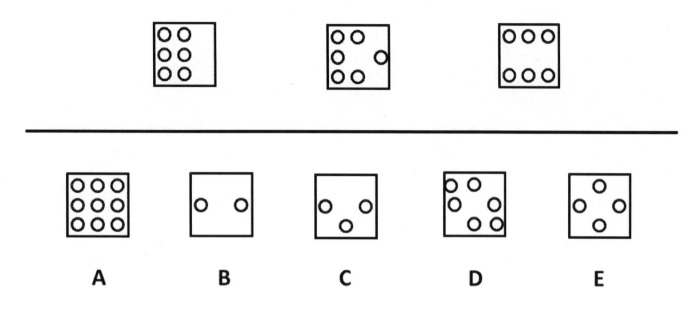

A   B   C   D   E

8.

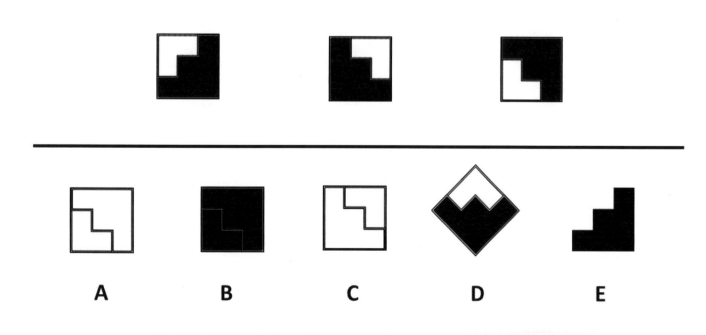

A   B   C   D   E

9.

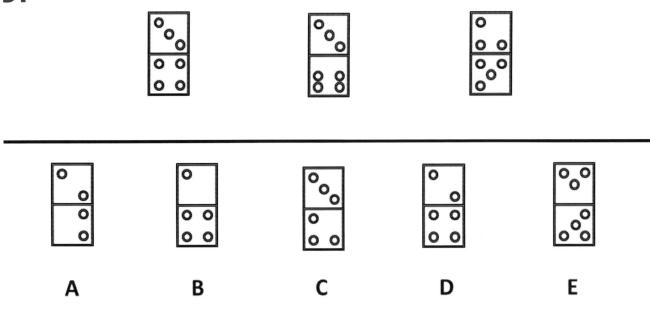

A   **B**   **C**   **D**   **E**

10.

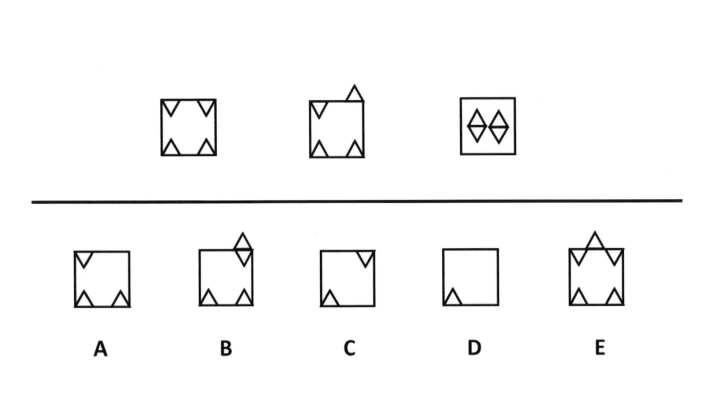

A   **B**   **C**   **D**   **E**

11.

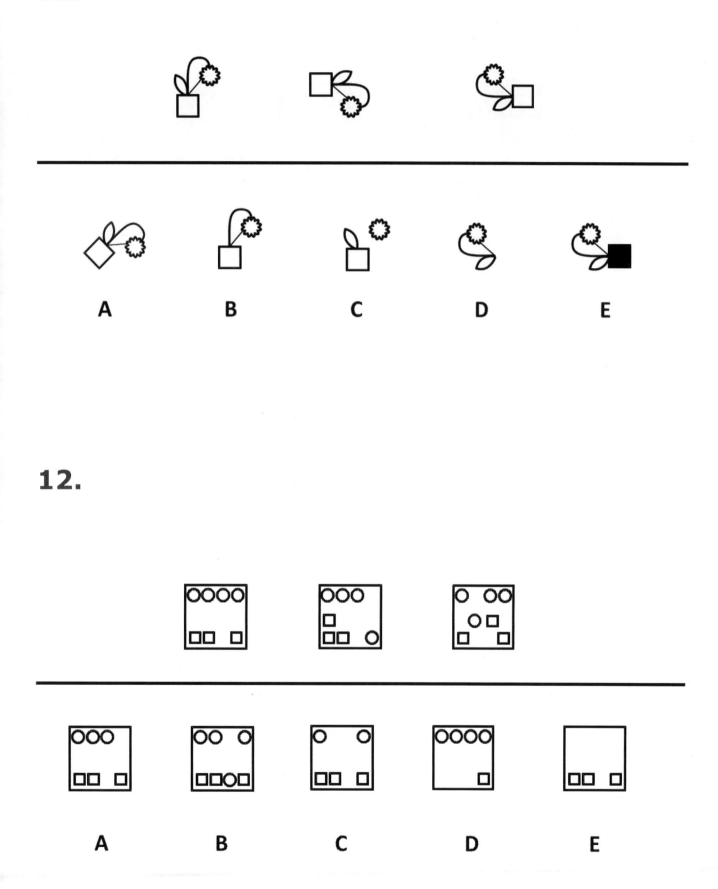

12.

13.

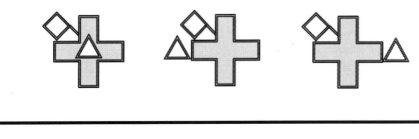

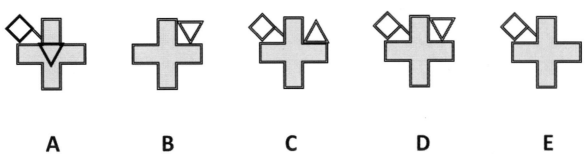

| A | B | C | D | E |

14.

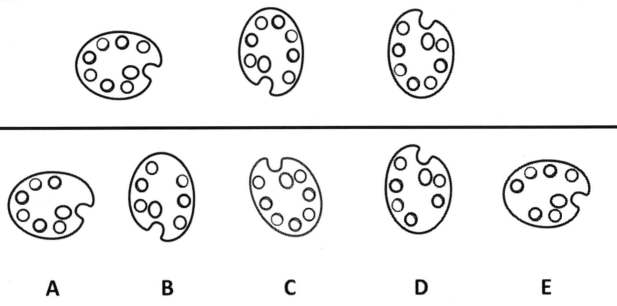

| A | B | C | D | E |

15.

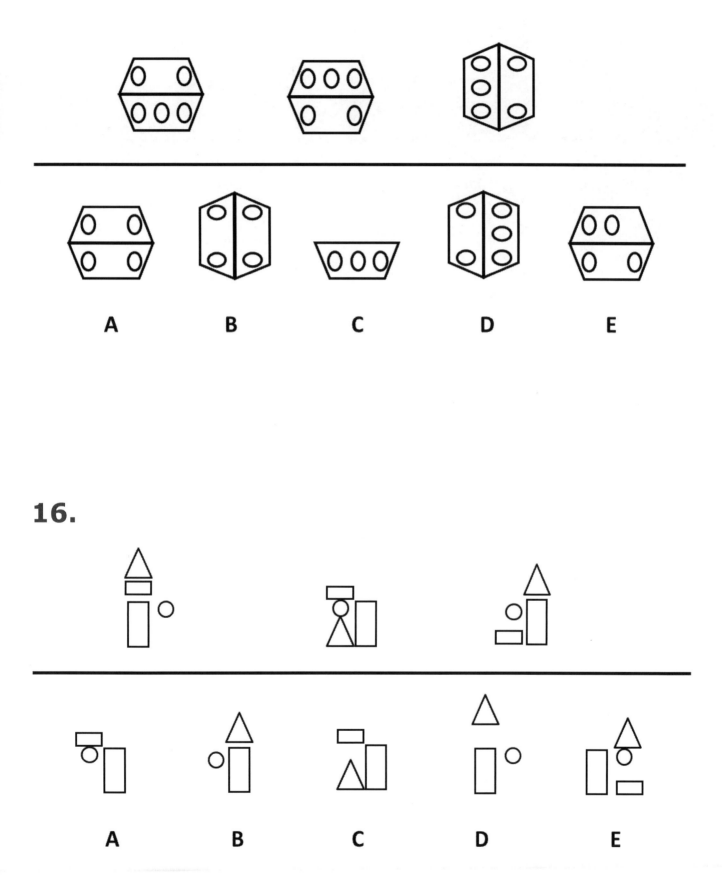

A   B   C   D   E

16.

A   B   C   D   E

17.

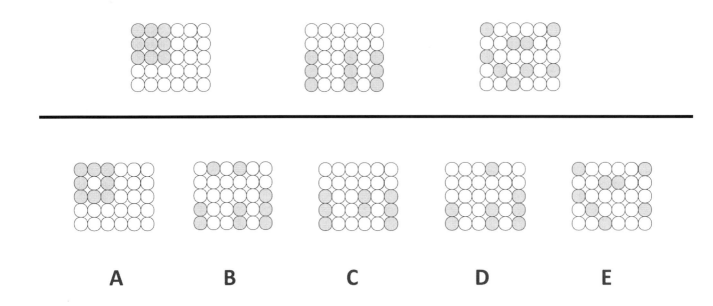

A   **B**   **C**   **D**   **E**

18.

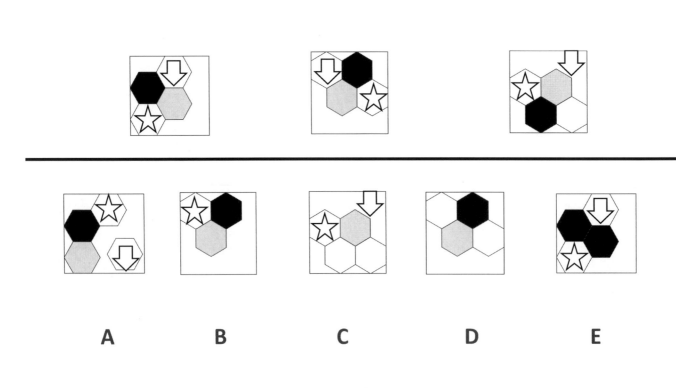

A   **B**   **C**   **D**   **E**

19.

A   **B**   **C**   **D**   **E**

20.

 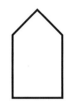 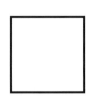  

A   **B**   **C**   **D**   **E**

21.

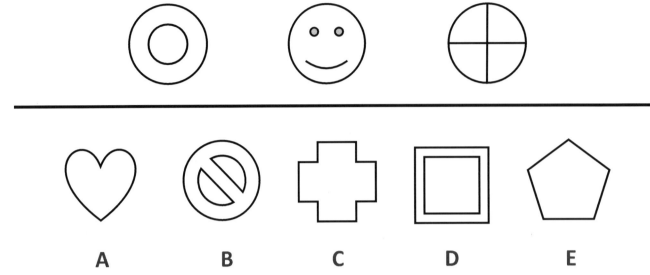

22.

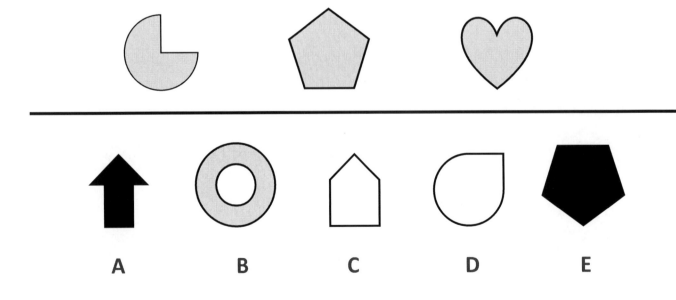

Paper Folding

1.

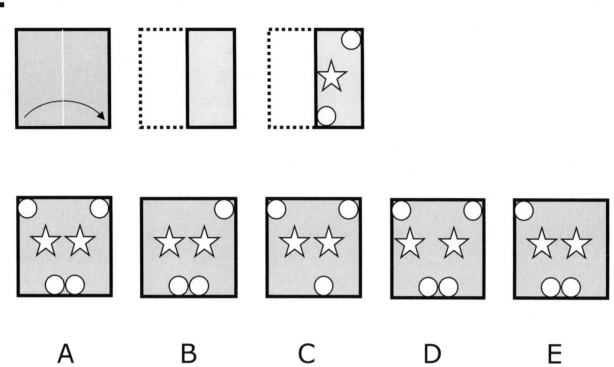

A   B   C   D   E

2.

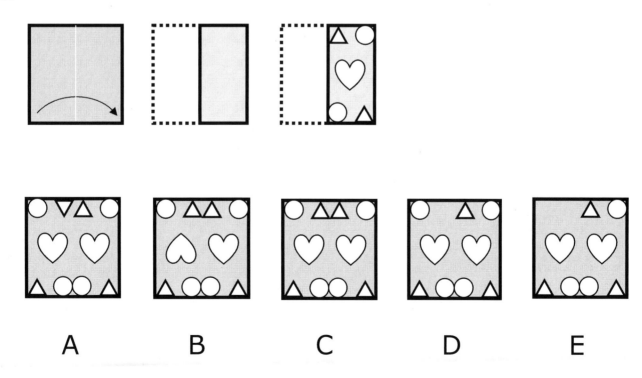

A   B   C   D   E

3.

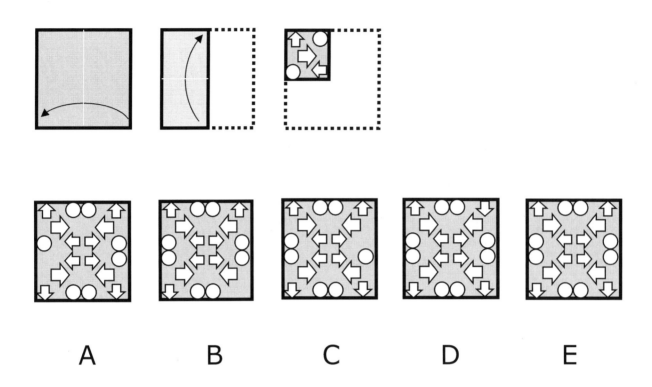

A   B   C   D   E

4.

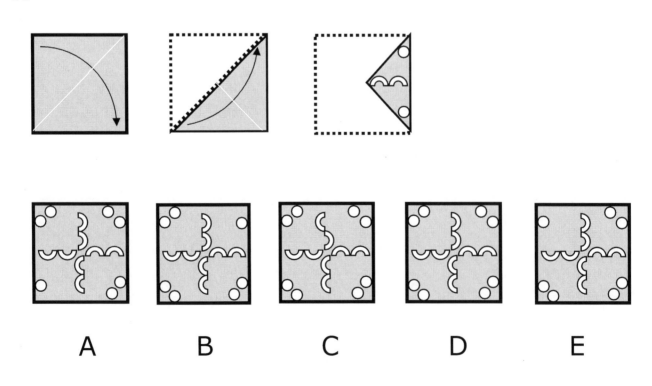

A   B   C   D   E

5.

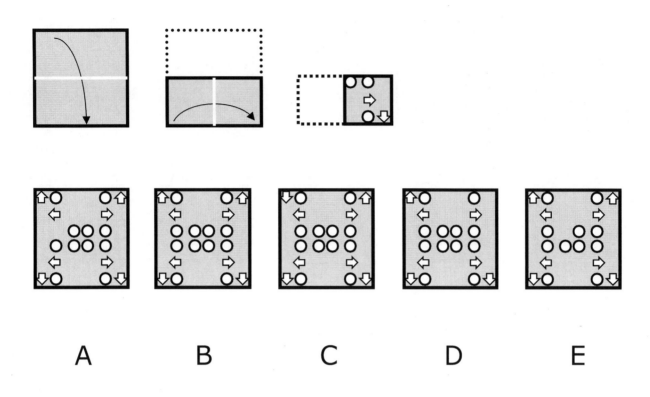

A   B   C   D   E

6.

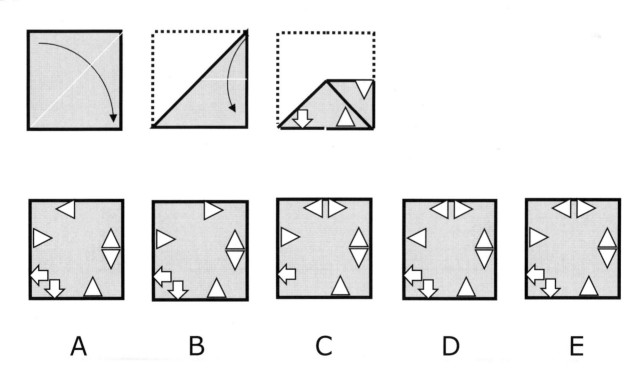

A   B   C   D   E

7.

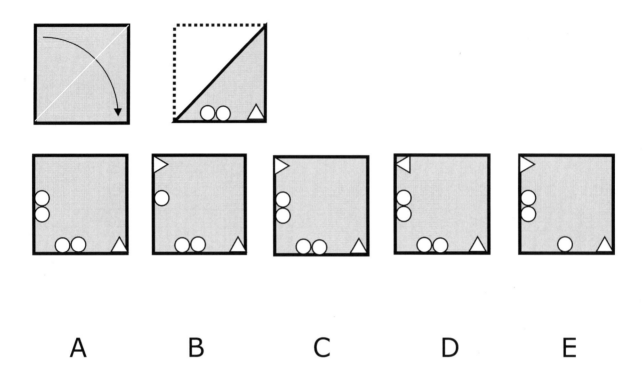

A   B   C   D   E

8.

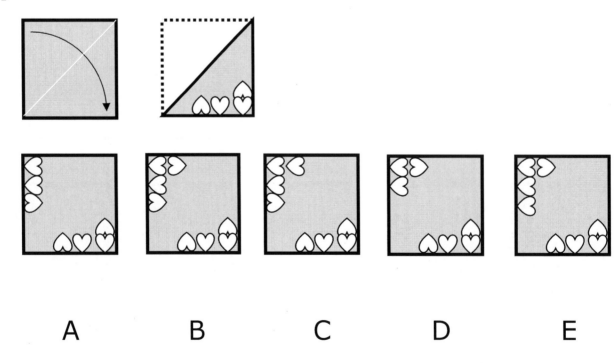

A   B   C   D   E

9.

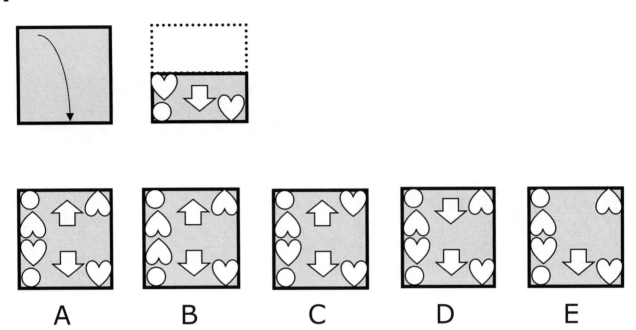

10.

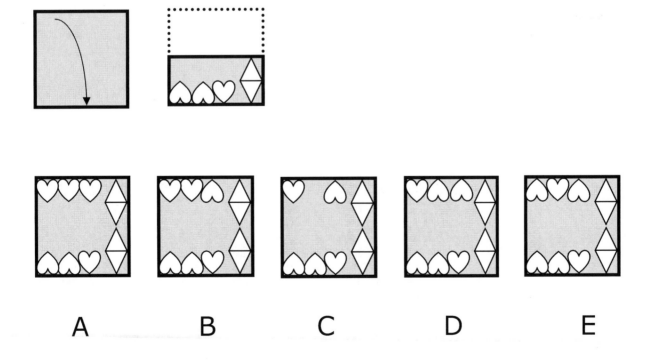

11.

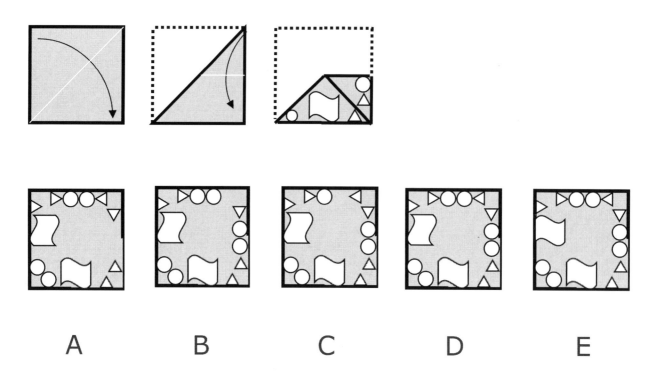

A   B   C   D   E

12.

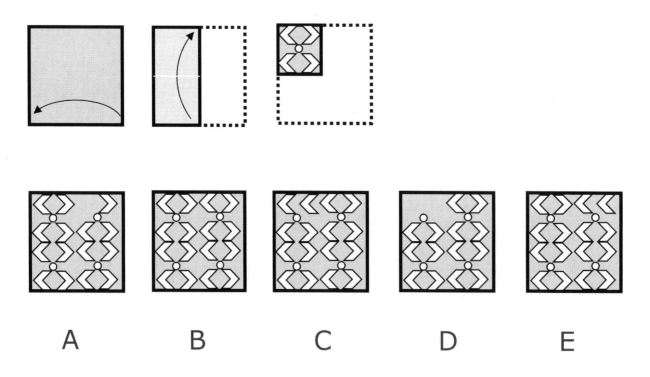

A   B   C   D   E

13.

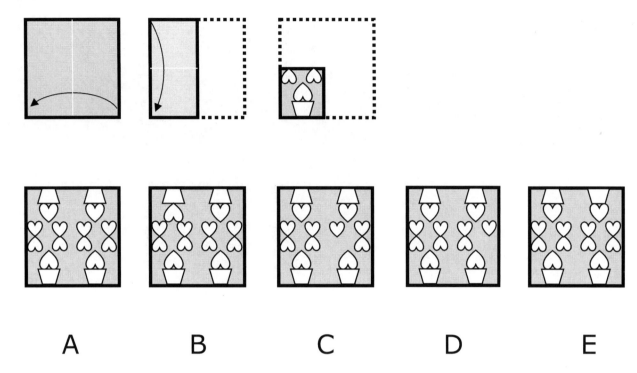

A   B   C   D   E

14.

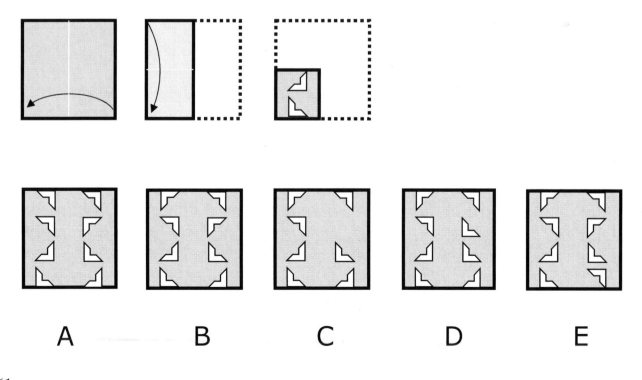

A   B   C   D   E

15.

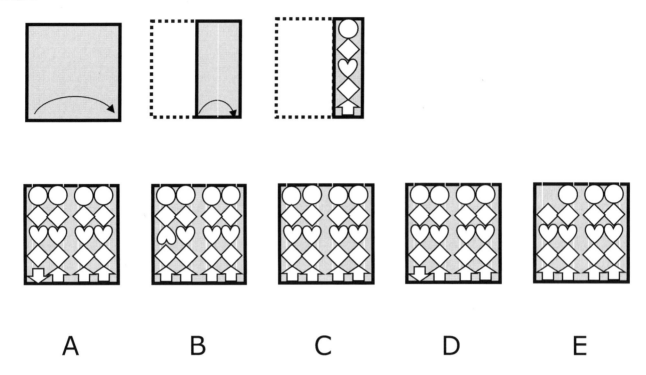

16.

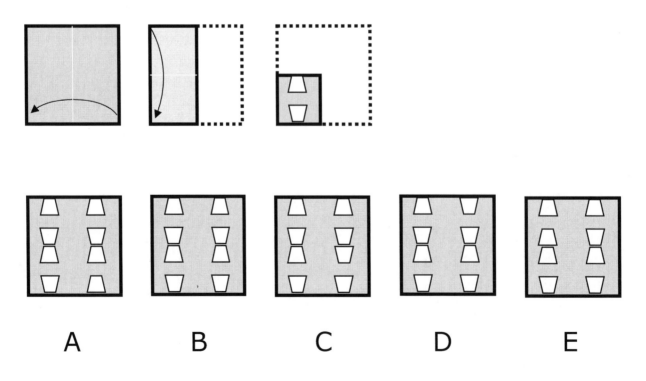

PRACTICE TEST 2 QUANTITATIVE BATTERY

Number Puzzle

1.

$$50 - ? = 38$$

A 13   **B** 12   **C** 11   **D** 10   **E** 21

2.

$$? + \blacklozenge = 29$$

$$\blacklozenge = 16$$

A 14   **B** 10   **C** 13   **D** 19   **E** 24

3.

$$? + 3 = \blacklozenge$$

$$\blacklozenge = 15$$

A 12   **B** 19   **C** 14   **D** 20   **E** 25

4.

$$? \times 2 = \blacklozenge + 15$$

$$\blacklozenge = 15$$

A 17 **B** 19 **C** 15 **D** 18 **E** 11

5.

$$? - 9 = \blacklozenge + 5$$

$$\blacklozenge = 91$$

A 91 **B** 101 **C** 22 **D** 105 **E** 102

6.

$$17 + 9 = 35 - ?$$

A 12 **B** 45 **C** 10 **D** 6 **E** 9

7.

$$36 = 68 - 15 - ?$$

A 10   **B** 28   **C** 31   **D** 17   **E** 10

8.

$$26 = 42 - 11 - ?$$

A 5   **B** 15   **C** 18   **D** 10   **E** 2

9. $$102 = 36 + 5 + ?$$

A 31   **B** 61   **C** 22   **D** 3   **E** 21

10.

$$99 - 33 = 100 - ?$$

A 14   **B** 31   **C** 32   **D** 34   **E** 18

11.

$$18 + 26 = 62 - ?$$

A 11   **B** 4   **C** 29   **D** 51   **E** 18

12.

$$85 - 43 = 100 - ?$$

A 58   **B** 31   **C** 22   **D** 31   **E** 12

13.

$$? = \blacklozenge + 44$$

$$\blacklozenge = 22$$

A 51   **B** 42   **C** 66   **D** 65   **E** 21

14.

$$? = \blacklozenge \times 5$$

$$\blacklozenge = 8$$

A 40   **B** 4   **C** 41   **D** 45   **E** 21

15.

$$? = \blacklozenge \times 8$$

$$\blacklozenge = 9$$

A 79　　**B** 18　　**C** 31　　**D** 72　　**E** 12

16.

$$? = \blacklozenge - 3$$

$$19 = \blacklozenge + \bullet$$

$$\bullet = 7$$

A 12　　**B** 9　　**C** 18　　**D** 19　　**E** 10

Number Analogies

1.

[11 → 20]   [8 → 17]   [17 → ?]

A 26   **B** 15   **C** 12   **D** 4   **E** 18

2.

[31 → 93]   [6 → 18]   [8 → ?]

A 23   **B** 11   **C** 21   **D** 29   **E** 24

3.

[42 → 36]   [19 → 13]   [88 → ?]

A 91   **B** 82   **C** 75   **D** 35   **E** 31

4.

[77 → 11]   [84 → 12]   [91 → ?]

A 75   **B** 13   **C** 61   **D** 79   **E** 11

5.

[6 → 23]   [7 → 27]   [9 → ?]

A 31   **B** 18   **C** 35   **D** 21   **E** 29

6.

[4 → 52]   [2 → 26]   [5 → ?]

A 65   **B** 85   **C** 21   **D** 12   **E** 74

7.

[9 → 45]   [11 → 55]   [8 → ?]

A 43   **B** 50   **C** 41   **D** 10   **E** 40

8.

[89 → 76]   [39 → 26]   [40 → ?]

A 27   **B** 21   **C** 18   **D** 1   **E** 12

9.

[104 → 26]   [56 → 14]   [64 → ?]

A 4   **B** 22   **C** 23   **D** 18   **E** 16

10.

[26 → 34]   [22 → 30]   [16 → ?]

A 21   **B** 12   **C** 119   **D** 31   **E** 24

11.

[96 → 12]   [16 → 2]   [112 → ?]

A 12   **B** 21   **C** 14   **D** 51   **E** 90

12.

[3 → 36]   [6 → 72]   [8 → ?]

A 96   **B** 66   **C** 46   **D** 31   **E** 15

13.
[105 → 35]   [69 → 23]   [99 → ?]

A 21   **B** 5   **C** 61   **D** 33   **E** 31

14.
[22 → 10]   [65 → 53]   [91 → ?]

A 99   **B** 79   **C** 78   **D** 18   **E** 29

15.
[35 → 28]   [46 → 39]   [65 → ?]

A 58   **B** 47   **C** 52   **D** 59   **E** 41

16.
[19 → 57]   [15 → 45]   [41 → ?]

A 110   **B** 123   **C** 49   **D** 600   **E** 134

17.

[78 → 13]   [90 → 15]   [96 → ?]

A 16   **B** 19   **C** 31   **D** 21   **E** 25

18.

[8 → 46]   [3 → 16]   [11 → ?]

A 25   **B** 16   **C** 31   **D** 64   **E** 84

Number Series

1.

28   **33**   **38**   **43**   **?**

A 20   **B** 21   **C** 20   **D** 90   **E** 48

2.

100   **94**   **88**   **82**   **76**   **?**

A 15   **B** 16   **C** 70   **D** 67   **E** 59

3.

60   **55**   **59**   **54**   **58**   **?**

A 43   **B** 84   **C** 49   **D** 53   **E** 10

4.

11   **26**   **41**   **56**   **71**   **86**   **101**   **?**

A 390   **B** 41   **C** 55   **D** 212   **E** 116

5.

      19   **25**   **32**   **40**   **?**

A 45   **B** 11   **C** 36   **D** 49   **E** 31

6.

      16   **11**   **14**   **9**   **12**   **7**   **?**

A 10   **B** 15   **C** 22   **D** 25   **E** 11

7.

      21   **1**   **21**   **1**   **21**   **?**

A 2   **B** 13   **C** 1   **D** 5   **E** 9

8.

      36   **29**   **33**   **26**   **30**   **23**   **?**

A 51   **B** 27   **C** 12   **D** 18   **E** 21

9.

| 64 | 58 | 52 | 46 | 40 | ? |

A 35   **B** 31   **C** 32   **D** 34   **E** 38

10.

| 5 | 13 | 15 | 23 | 25 | 33 | ? |

A 81   **B** 22   **C** 10   **D** 11   **E** 35

11.

| 22 | 24 | 26 | 28 | 30 | 32 | ? |

A 42   **B** 34   **C** 26   **D** 49   **E** 51

12.

| 2 | 19 | 36 | 53 | 70 | 87 | ? |

A 81   **B** 104   **C** 86   **D** 101   **E** 102

13.

9 12 15 18 21 24 ?

A 16 **B** 12 **C** 26 **D** 37 **E** 27

14.

0.5 1.1 1.7 2.3 2.9 3.5 ?

A 4.1 **B** 2.1 **C** 7.1 **D** 3.5 **E** 7.3

15.

0.08 0.17 0.26 0.35 0.44 ?

A 0.01 **B** 0.54 **C** 0.53 **D** 0.93 **E** 0.1

16.

105 97 89 81 73 65 ?

A 51 **B** 58 **C** 56 **D** 57 **E** 39

17.

    9.2   10   10.8   11.6   12.4   13,2   ?

A 11   **B** 9.5   **C** 14   **D** 11.6   **E** 50.2

18.

    12   11.95   11.9   11.85   11.8   11,75   ?

A 11.7   **B** 31.8   **C** 7.8   **D** 7.32   **E** 8.3

ANSWER KEY TEST 2

Verbal Analogies Practice Test
p.116

1.
Answer: option B
Explanation: a pentagon is any five-sided polygon; a dodecagon is a twelve-sided polygon

2.
Answer: option A
Explanation: the first 2 letters of the word "centimeter" are "ce"; the first 2 letters of the word "weight" are "we".

3.
Answer: option C
Explanation: synonyms.

4.
Answer: option D
Explanation: denim is a fabric made from cotton; linen is a fabric made from flax.

5.
Answer: option B
Explanation: antonyms.

6.
Answer: option E
Explanation: a seraphim is an angel; a nymph is a maiden.

7.
Answer: option B
Explanation: tree becomes ree when the "t" is removed, and table becomes able when the "t" is removed.

8.

Answer: option E

Explanation: to segregate is an antonym of to unify; to repair is an antonym of to damage.

9.

Answer: option C

Explanation: an opossum is an example of a marsupial; a seal is an example of a mammal.

10.

Answer: option A

Explanation: a cicada is a type of insect: a fox is a type of canine.

11.

Answer: option B

Explanation: geology is the study of rocks; ornithology is the study of birds.

12.

Answer: option D

Explanation: a purse is used to hold money; an urn is used to hold ashes.

13.

Answer: option C

Explanation: a ribbon is used to decorate a present; icing is used to decorate a cake.

14.

Answer: option A

Explanation: a whale lives in the ocean; a slug lives on land.

15.
Answer: option D
Explanation: a spoke is part of a wheel; a word is part of a sentence.

16.
Answer: option A
Explanation: an engine is part of a car; a vamp is part of a shoe.

17.
Answer: option B
Explanation: a drive is an action in golf; a serve is an action in tennis.

18.
Answer: option E
Explanation: a pestle is a tool for grinding; a saw is a tool for cutting.

19.
Answer: option C
Explanation: a stigma is a part of flower; an atom is a part of a molecule.

20.
Answer: option B
Explanation: a scalpel is used to make an incision; a spatula is used for lifting.

21.
Answer: option A
Explanation: an atlas contains maps; a dictionary is a book containing definitions.

22.
Answer: option B
Explanation: a bonsai tree is grown in a pot; a sequoia grows in a forest.

23.
Answer: option E
Explanation: comical is an antonym for pathetic, and early is an antonym for late.

24.
Answer: option D
Explanation: a mechanic works at a garage; a professor works at a college.

Verbal Classification Practice Test
P 122

1.
Answer: option E
Explanation: nucleus, neutron, proton and electron are part of an atom.

2.
Answer: option D
Explanation: body, ability, academy and city are words that end with the letter y.

3.
Answer: option B
Explanation: frame, saddle, wheel and pedal are bicycle parts.

4.
Answer: option A
Explanation: crown, root, pulp and cementum are part of a tooth.

5.
Answer: option A
Explanation: stern, bow, anchor and sail are parts of a ship.

6.
Answer: option C
Explanation: date, closing, body and signature are parts of a letter.

7.
Answer: option E
Explanation: Fuji, Gala, Golden delicious and Granny Smith are types of apple.

8.
Answer: option B
Explanation: personal, relative, possessive, and indefinite are types of pronouns.

9.
Answer: option D
Explanation: iguanodon, allosaurus, carnotaurus and albertosaurus are types of dinosaurs.

10.
Answer: option A
Explanation: akasa, bamboo, teak and pine are types of wood.

11.
Answer: option E
Explanation: political, physical, topographic, and geologic are types of maps.

12.
Answer: option B
Explanation: incisors, canine, molar and premolar are types of teeth.

13.
Answer: option B
Explanation: histogram, line, bar and pie are types of graphs.

14.
Answer: option A
Explanation: grenade, crossbow, sword and torpedo are types of weapons.

15.
Answer: option E
Explanation: imperative, declarative, exclamatory and interrogative are types of sentences.

16.
Answer: option C
Explanation: A, C, D and K are types of vitamins.

17.
Answer: option D
Explanation: medulla, hypothalamus, cerebellum and pituitary gland are parts of the brain.

18.
Answer: option A
Explanation: keyboard, camera, screen and touchpad are parts of laptop computer

19.
Answer: option E
Explanation: lenses, bridge, nose pads and rims are parts of eyeglasses.

20.
Answer: option B
Explanation: clavicle, scapula, sternum and radius are bones of the body.

Sentence Completion Practice Test
p.127

1.
Answer: option C
Explanation: hollow= a depression in something.

2.
Answer: option D
Explanation: jealous= feeling or showing an envious resentment of someone.

3.
Answer: option A
Explanation: straight= not curved or bent.

4.
Answer: option D
Explanation: produce = to create something.

5.
Answer: option B
Explanation: frazzled = showing the effects of exhaustion or strain.

6.
Answer: option A
Explanation: profitable= yielding profit or financial gain.

7.
Answer: option E
Explanation: study= the devotion of time and attention to gaining knowledge
.

8.
Answer: option B
Explanation: place = a specific area or region of the world.

9.
Answer: option C
Explanation: submarine= existing under the surface of the sea.

10.
Answer: option D
Explanation: hidden= kept out of sight.

11.
Answer: option B
Explanation: helping = to provide with something that is useful or necessary.

12.
Answer: option C
Explanation: place= a specific area.

13.
Answer: option C
Explanation: follow = come after in time or order.

14.
Answer: option E
Explanation: political= a political border is an imaginary line separating one political unit, such as a country or state, from another.

15.
Answer: option C
Explanation: vertically= at right angles to a horizontal plane.

16.
Answer: option E
Explanation: allow = let have or do something.

17.
Answer: option B
Explanation: stressed = experiencing mental or emotional strain or tension.

18.
Answer: option A
Explanation: leavening agent = raising agent

19.
Answer: option C
Explanation: sound = something that you can hear.

20.
Answer: option B
Explanation: clean = uncontaminated.

Figure Matrices Practice Test
p.136

1.
Answer: option A
Explanation: the outer figure becomes gray; the inner figure becomes white.

2.
Answer: option D
Explanation: the outer figure is flipped vertically.

3.
Answer: option E
Explanation: the circle in the center is eliminated.

4.
Answer: option B
Explanation: the black triangle is eliminated and the figure becomes gray.

5.
Answer: option A
Explanation: the black figure becomes white; the top figure is flipped vertically.

6.
Answer: option C
Explanation: only the left side of the triangle is left; the black heart becomes white.

7.
Answer: option C
Explanation: the figure rotates by 90 degrees counterclockwise.

8.
Answer: option A
Explanation: the inner figure rotates by 90 degrees clockwise.

9.
Answer: option B
Explanation: the middle element is deleted; the top element becomes white.

10.
Answer: option E
Explanation: the figure becomes gray; a black circle is added in the lower right corner.

11.
Answer: option E
Explanation: the left figure rotates by 45 degrees clockwise; 4 black circles are added.

12.
Answer: option E
Explanation: the figure rotates by 45 degrees clockwise.

13.
Answer: option B
Explanation: the circle in the center of the figure is eliminated.

14.
Answer: option C
Explanation: the central figure becomes white; the 2 elements along the left diagonal become black.

15.
Answer: option D
Explanation: the figure rotates by 90 degrees counterclockwise.

16.
Answer: option A
Explanation: the outer figure becomes gray; the inside figure becomes black.

17.
Answer: option B
Explanation: the outer figure turns black; the arrow is flipped vertically.

18.
Answer: option D
Explanation: the top element turns gray; the bottom element turns white; the black circle moves to the top.

19.
Answer: option A
Explanation: the figure is flipped vertically; the bottom and top figures become gray.

20.
Answer: option C
Explanation: the cross turns gray; the circle is eliminated.

21.
Answer: option A
Explanation: the flag moves to the right; the inner figure becomes a triangle; the main figure doesn't change.

22.
Answer: option E
Explanation: the element on the left becomes white and it is placed in a circle.

Figure Classification Practice Test
p.144

1.
Answer: option B
Explanation: combos of a black 5-pointed star, a white 4-pointed star, and a gray 6-pointed star.

2.
Answer: option A
Explanation: same figure, consisting of 2 squares, each containing a triangle, rotated.

3.
Answer: option D
Explanation: combos of a white 4-pointed star, a white circle, a black triangle pointing up, a black arrow pointing right.

4.
Answer: option C
Explanation: each figure contains an equal inside shape and an equal above shape.

5.
Answer: option A
Explanation: combos of a white square and 4 white circles.

6.
Answer: option D
Explanation: figures divided into 4 equal parts.

7.

Answer: option D
Explanation: in each square, there are 6 white circles.

8.

Answer: option D
Explanation: same figure rotated.

9.

Answer: option E
Explanation: in the top square there are 3 white circles; in the bottom square there are 4 white circles.

10.

Answer: option B
Explanation: combos of a square and 4 triangles.

11.

Answer: option A
Explanation: same figure, rotated.

12.

Answer: option B
Explanation: in each square, there are 4 circles and 3 squares.

13.

Answer: option C
Explanation: combos of a grey cross, a white flag pointing left, and a white triangle pointing up.

14.

Answer: option C
Explanation: same figure rotated
.

15.
Answer: option D
Explanation: combos of 2 trapezoids and 5 oval shapes.

16.
Answer: option E
Explanation: combos of a white triangle, 2 white rectangles and a white circle.

17.
Answer: option B
Explanation: 21 white circles and 9 grey circles.

18.
Answer: option A
Explanation: combos of 2 white hexagons, a black hexagon, a grey hexagon, a white star and a white arrow pointing down.

19.
Answer: option C
Explanation: combos of 2 black hearts, a grey heart, a white heart and a white star. The star is always inside the white heart.

20.
Answer: option A
Explanation: 6-sided figures.

21.
Answer: option B
Explanation: circular shapes.

22.
Answer: option B
Explanation: grey figures.

Paper Folding Practice Test

p.155

1.
Answer: option A

2.
Answer: option C

3.
Answer: option E

4.
Answer: option D

5.
Answer: option B

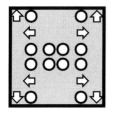

6.
Answer: option E

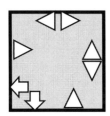

7
Answer: option C

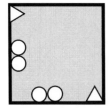

8.
Answer: option B

9.
Answer: option A

10.
Answer: option B

11.
Answer: option D

12.
Answer: option B

13.
Answer: option A

14.
Answer: option B

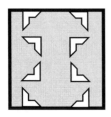

15.
Answer: option C

16.
Answer: option B

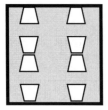

Number Puzzle Practice Test
p.164

1.
Answer: option B
Explanation: 50-12=38; 38=38

2.
Answer: option C
Explanation: 13+16=29; 29=29

3.
Answer: option A
Explanation: 12+3=15; 15=15

4.
Answer: option C
Explanation: 15X2=15+15; 30=30

5.
Answer: option D
Explanation: 105-9=91+5; 96=96

6.
Answer: option E
Explanation: 17+9=35-9; 26=26

7.
Answer: option D
Explanation: 36=68-15-17; 36=36

8.
Answer: option A
Explanation: 26=42-11 - 5; 26=26

9.
Answer: option B
Explanation: $102=36+5+61$; $102=102$

10.
Answer: option D
Explanation: $99-33=100-34$; $66=66$

11.
Answer: option E
Explanation: $18+26=62-18$; $44=44$

12.
Answer: option A
Explanation: $85-43=100-58$; $42=42$

13.
Answer: option C
Explanation: $66=22+44$; $66=66$

14.
Answer: option A
Explanation: $40=8X5$; $40=40$

15.
Answer: option D
Explanation: $72=9X8$; $72=72$

16.
Answer: option B
Explanation: ◆ $= 19-7$; ◆ $=12$; $9=12-3$; $9=9$

Number Analogies Practice Test
p.169

1.
Answer: option A
Explanation: 11+9=20   8+9=17   17+9=26

2.
Answer: option E
Explanation: 31X3=93   6X3=18   8X3=24

3.
Answer: option B
Explanation: 42-6=36   19-6=13   88-6=82

4.
Answer: option B
Explanation: 77:7=11   84:7=12   91:7=13

5.
Answer: option C
Explanation: 6X4=24; 24-1=23   7X4=28; 28-1=27   9X4=36; 36-1=35

6.
Answer: option A
Explanation: 4X13=52   2X13=26   5X13=65

7.
Answer: option E
Explanation: 9X5=45; 11X5=55; 8X5=40;

8.
Answer: option A
Explanation: 89-13=76   39-13=26   40-13=27

9.
Answer: option E
Explanation: 104:4=26   56:4=14   64:4=16

10.
Answer: option E
Explanation: 26+8=34   22+8=30   16+8=24

11.
Answer: option C
Explanation: 96:8=12   16:8=2   112:8=14

12.
Answer: option A
Explanation: 3X12=36   6X12=72   8X12=96

13.
Answer: option D
Explanation: 105:3=35   69:3=23   99:3=33

14.
Answer: option B
Explanation: 22-12=10   65-12=53   91-12=79

15.
Answer: option A
Explanation: 35-7=28   46-7=39   65-7=58

16.
Answer: option B
Explanation: 19X3=57   15X3=45   41X3=123

17.
Answer: option A
Explanation: 78:6=13   90:6=15   96:6=16

18.
Answer: option D
Explanation: 8X6=48; 48-2=46   3X6=18; 18-2=16
                 11X6=66; 66-2=64

Number Series Practice Test
p.174

1.
Answer: option E
Explanation: +5, +5, +5, +5, etc.

2.
Answer: option C
Explanation: -6, -6, -6, -6, -6, etc.

3.
Answer: option D
Explanation: -5, +4, -5, +4, -5

4.
Answer: option E
Explanation: +15, +15, +15, +15, +15, +15, +15, etc.

5.
Answer: option D
Explanation: +6, +7, +8, +9, etc.

6.
Answer: option A
Explanation: -5, +3, -5, +3, -5, +3, etc.

7.
Answer: option C
Explanation: -20, +20, -20, +20, -20, etc.

8.
Answer: option B
Explanation: -7, +4, -7, +4, -7, +4, etc.

9.
Answer: option D
Explanation: -6, -6, -6, -6, -6, etc.

10.
Answer: option E
Explanation: +8, +2, +8, +2, +8, +2, etc.

11.
Answer: option B
Explanation: +2, +2, +2, 2, +2, +2, etc.

12.
Answer: option B
Explanation: +17, +17, +17, +17, +17, +17, etc.

13.
Answer: option E
Explanation: +3, +3, +3, +3, etc.

14.
Answer: option A
Explanation: +0.6, +0.6, +0.6, +0.6, +0.6, +0.6, etc.

15.
Answer: option C
Explanation: +0.09, +0.09, +0.09, +0.09, +0.09, +0.09, etc.

16.
Answer: option D
Explanation: -8, -8, -8, -8, -8, -8, etc.

17.
Answer: option C
Explanation: +0.8, +0.8, +0.8, +0.8, +0.8, +0.8, etc.

18.
Answer: option A
Explanation: -0.05, -0.05, -0.05, -0.05, -0.05, -0.05, etc.

HOW TO DOWNLOAD 54 BONUS QUESTIONS

Thank you for reading this book, we hope you really enjoyed it and found it very helpful.

PLEASE LEAVE US A REVIEW ON THE WEBSITE WHERE YOU PURCHASED THIS BOOK!

By leaving a review, you give us the opportunity to improve our work.

A GIFT FOR YOU!

FREE ONLINE ACCESS TO 54 BONUS PRACTICE QUESTIONS.

Follow this link:

https://www.skilledchildren.com/free-download-cogat-level-10.php

You will find a PDF to download: please insert this PASSWORD: 200017

Nicole Howard and the SkilledChildren.com Team

www.skilledchildren.com

The Best Collection of Books for Child Brain Development.

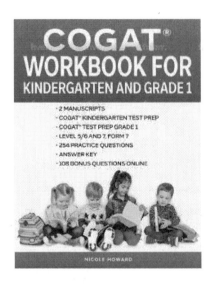

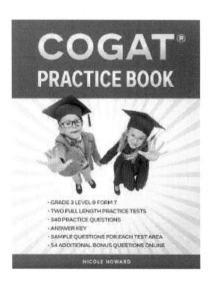

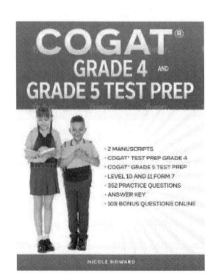

COGAT®
GRADE 5 TEST PREP

- GRADE 5 LEVEL 11 FORM 7
- ONE FULL-LENGTH PRACTICE TEST
- 176 PRACTICE QUESTIONS
- ANSWER KEY
- SAMPLE QUESTIONS FOR EACH TEST AREA
- 54 ADDITIONAL BONUS QUESTIONS ONLINE

NICOLE HOWARD

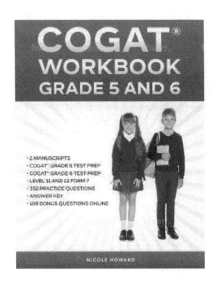

COGAT®
WORKBOOK
GRADE 5 AND 6

- 2 MANUSCRIPTS
- COGAT® GRADE 5 TEST PREP
- COGAT® GRADE 6 TEST PREP
- LEVEL 11 AND 12 FORM 7
- 352 PRACTICE QUESTIONS
- ANSWER KEY
- 108 BONUS QUESTIONS ONLINE

NICOLE HOWARD

COGAT®
GRADE 6 & 7/8 TEST PREP

- 2 MANUSCRIPTS
- COGAT® GRADE 6 TEST PREP
- COGAT® GRADE 7/8 TEST PREP
- LEVEL 12, 13, AND 14 FORM 7
- 352 PRACTICE QUESTIONS
- ANSWER KEY
- 108 BONUS QUESTIONS ONLINE

NICOLE HOWARD

COGAT®
GRADE 7/8 TEST PREP

- GRADE 7/8 LEVEL 13/14 FORM 7
- ONE FULL-LENGTH PRACTICE TEST
- 176 PRACTICE QUESTIONS
- ANSWER KEY
- SAMPLE QUESTIONS FOR EACH TEST AREA
- 54 ADDITIONAL BONUS QUESTIONS ONLINE

NICOLE HOWARD

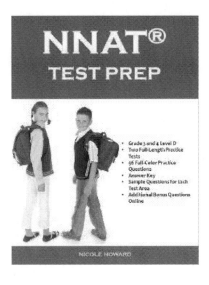

NNAT®
TEST PREP

- Grade 3 and 4 Level D
- Two Full-Length Practice Tests
- 96 Full-Color Practice Questions
- Answer Key
- Sample Questions for Each Test Area
- Additional Bonus Questions Online

NICOLE HOWARD

GIFTED CHILDREN
WORKBOOK
GRADE K

ABC

- CRITICAL THINKING FOR YOUNG CHILDREN
- SUPPORT FOR COGAT®, NNAT® AND OLSAT® TESTING
- 188 COLORFUL BRAIN GAMES
- ANSWER KEY
- 54 BONUS QUESTIONS ONLINE

NICOLE HOWARD

GIFTED CHILDREN
WORKBOOK
GRADE 1

ABC

- CRITICAL THINKING FOR YOUNG CHILDREN
- SUPPORT FOR COGAT®, NNAT® AND OLSAT® TESTING
- 192 COLORFUL BRAIN GAMES
- ANSWER KEY
- 54 BONUS QUESTIONS ONLINE

NICOLE HOWARD

OLSAT®
GRADE 2 TEST PREP

- GRADE 2, LEVEL C
- TWO FULL-LENGTH PRACTICE TESTS
- 120 PRACTICE QUESTIONS
- ANSWER KEY
- SAMPLE QUESTIONS FOR EACH TEST AREA
- 30 ADDITIONAL BONUS QUESTIONS ONLINE

NICOLE HOWARD

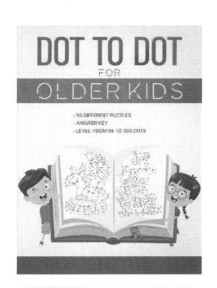

DOT TO DOT
FOR
OLDER KIDS

- 50 DIFFERENT PUZZLES
- ANSWER KEY
- LEVEL: FROM 94 TO 368 DOTS

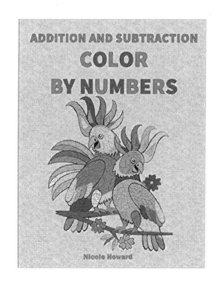

Made in the USA
Coppell, TX
06 September 2023